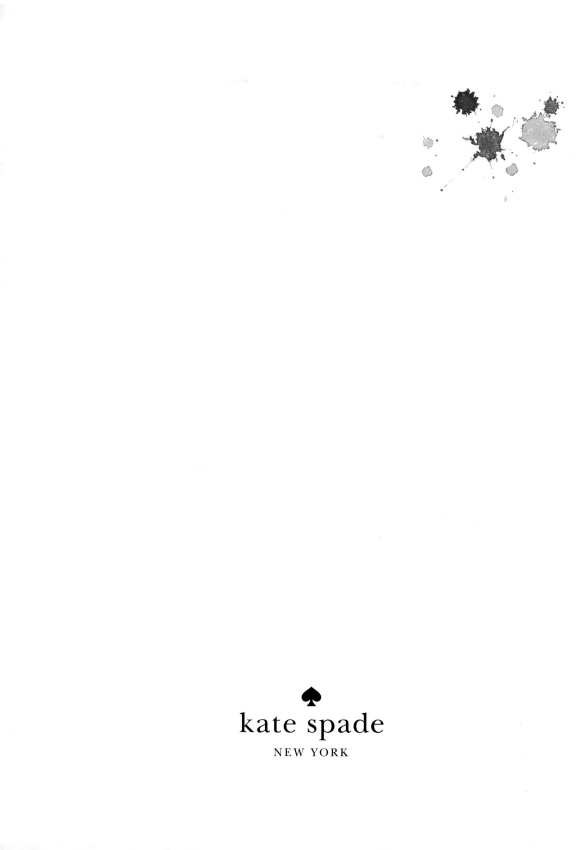

kate spade
NEW YORK

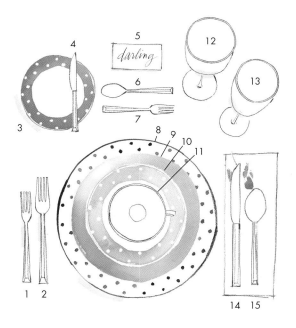

darling

1. salad fork
2. dinner fork
3. bread plate
4. bread knife
5. placecard
(using nickname in lieu of proper name)
6. ice cream spoon
7. cake fork

8. charger
9. dinner plate
10. saucer as salad plate
11. teacup as soup bowl
12. wine glass
13. water glass
14. knife
15. soup spoon

all in good taste

kate spade

NEW YORK

ABRAMS, NEW YORK

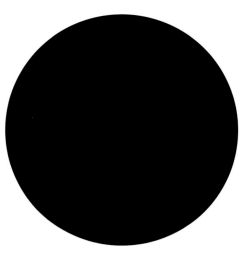

Editor: Holly Dolce and Rebecca Kaplan
Production Manager: Denise LaCongo

Library of Congress Control Number: 2014959566

ISBN: 978-1-4197-1787-1

Text copyright © 2015 kate spade new york

Printed and bound in China
10 9 8

Abrams books are available at special discounts when purchased in quan-
tity for premiums and promotions as well as fundraising or educational
use. Special editions can also be created to specification. For details,
contact specialsales@abramsbooks.com or the address below.

ABRAMS The Art of Books
195 Broadway, New York, NY 10007
abramsbooks.com

contents

there's nothing i love more than an evening at home hosting friends with my husband, simon, and our two dogs, stanley and lulu. they make our house a home. i'll make any excuse to put fresh flowers on the table, pop a bottle of bubbly and break out the fine china— whether it's for a chinese takeout or a homemade pot roast—and spark interesting conversation that trickles from the dining room to post-dinner chats in the garden over a delicious dessert.

my signature
sponge cake

INGREDIENTS

4 large eggs
179g castor sugar*
56g plain flour*
35g corn flour*
1 level tsp baking powder
whipped cream
homemade raspberry jam

*this converts roughly to 6 oz castor sugar, 2 oz plain flour, 1 oz corn flour

DIRECTIONS

preheat oven to 350°f. line two 8-inch sponge tins. sieve flour, baking powder and corn flour together. into two separate bowls, separate eggs and whisk egg whites until stiff. whisk in sugar. whisk egg yolks then add them to the egg white and sugar mixture and whisk altogether. fold in the flour, baking powder and corn flour, mix until smooth and divide batter between the two tins. bake for 25-30 minutes, until the cakes are risen, golden and feel springy to the touch. remove and let cool for a few minutes, then release by running a knife around the edges of the tin.

place cakes on a wire rack to cool completely. sandwich with whipped cream and homemade raspberry jam.

Deborah

president & chief creative officer
kate spade new york

entert

if it doesn't go awry, then it isn't a party.

gracious notes for the spirited hostess

above all, remember that the secret to a memorable party is putting people in a good mood—everyone dancing, laughing, being witty, flirting and celebrating. and not sweating the small stuff.

dana,
it's safe to say i have never laughed so much in all my life. i think laughter may have even spilled out of the living room. (along with some champagne on your rug.) thank you for a wonderful evening!

kristen

Sophie,

last night's dinner was
a most unusual evening—
and all the more fun for it.
(next time we'll all be at least
semi-proficient at flambéing
our desserts.)

thank you for my new book!

xoxo,
me

setting the scene

make preparing for the party as fun as the big event, with charming twists and personal touches designed to surprise and delight.

pick one thing and do it en masse[1]:

▶ string a thousand fairy lights above the garden.
▶ put out one hundred pillar candles.
▶ cover a table in six tiered cake stands instead of one.
▶ coat a ceiling in helium balloons (or hang at least thirty).
▶ fill large hurricane vases with foil-wrapped chocolates.
▶ cluster three christmas trees together for the holidays.
▶ place one or two disco balls on the floor of every room to cast a slight shimmer on white walls.

then, around the house, add a few extra touches:

▶ replace overhead and lamp lightbulbs with flattering twenty-five-watt bulbs.
▶ put a discreet piece of tape over dimmer light switches once you've set the mood.
▶ write "hello gorgeous" on the bathroom mirror in red lipstick.
▶ hook nice wooden hangers on your shower rod to turn it into a coat check.
▶ place floating candles in the bathtub (if not using the bathtub rail as coat rack).
▶ lay a fancy ashtray outside for smokers.
▶ lightly perfume the air by simmering fruits and spices on the stove (orange, cinnamon and cloves in winter; lime, thyme and mint in summer).
▶ adorn the bathroom with a dish of mints, box of tissues, crisp hand towels, extra rolls of toilet paper, a fresh gardenia[2] in a bud vase and a chic bottle of liquid hand soap.

[1] any obscure, weird, vintage or hybrid thing you want, you can probably order from etsy.
[2] a gardenia is one of the world's most fragrant flowers.

"I DECORATE THE HOUSE TO THE GILLS. IT'S QUITE UNUSUAL BECAUSE WE HAVE ALL THESE TOYS THAT DANCE AND SING. PEOPLE DON'T LET ME PUT IT AWAY SO I KEEP IT ALL UP FOR MONTHS. I BELIEVE CHRISTMAS IS A STATE OF MIND." *iris apfel*

"thomas pynchon writes the best parties.[3] strobed journeys through california house parties and verbose manhattan apartment parties that form a snippet of longer conversations."

the party, as if it were inanimate after all, unwound like a clock's mainspring towards the edges of the chocolate room, seeking some easing of its own tension, some equilibrium. THOMAS PYNCHON *in his novel* V

"his parties are, after all, animate. they're not in the tradition of awkward literary parties, from proust to franzen, where the guests speak into wells of silence and look at each other as though pinned to boards."

SARAH MCNALLY, *owner of mcnally jackson books in new york city*

[3] these include a beatnik loft party in *slow learner*, a prank-filled dinner in *gravity's rainbow*, a dot-com bash in *bleeding edge*, a tupperware party in *the crying of lot 49*.

flowers

"beautiful flowers" can take on many forms. while a tightly packed vase of peonies has classic charm, peculiar plants—balls of succulents, purple mini pineapples or small cacti in lacquered or vintage pots—are conversation starters. blooms arranged *au naturel*, even a little wild and looking as if they had come from the field rather than the florist, can be an alluring punctuation to a formal matching set of china.

if you don't have the "right" vase, think outside it: grab an empty perfume bottle, graphically-interesting soup can, water glass or salad bowl; tie together a group of glass bottles with twine; hollow out a lightbulb and hook it on the wall with grosgrain ribbon.

flower market or deli?

the local bodega is convenient; blooms from the flower market take some planning to get, but last longer.

chop chop

trim stems in two groups: flowers that outline the rim of the vase should be just a bit longer than the vase itself; the ones in the center should be a tiny bit longer than those, to create a nicely rounded bouquet silhouette.

"pink peonies in a crystal bowl with gold dots"
DEBORAH LLOYD
our chief creative officer

white peonies and cornflowers
JACKIE KENNEDY
former first lady

a ball of succulents

tightly packed, monochromatic bodega carnations

✳ FILL YOUR VASE WITH WARM—NOT COLD—WATER TO ENCOURAGE YOUR FLOWERS TO DRINK UP.

a single lanky
stem of green
hydrangeas in
a tall, clear
liquor bottle

garden
roses,
peonies and
ranunculus

a bunch
of anemones
in different
shades

"freesia, peonies,
ranunculus, sweet peas
and wild roses,
plopped—low and wide—
into old french jam jars"
MARTHA WARD
stylist

goldenrod
and cosmos
RACHEL "BUNNY" MELLON
horticulturalist

tulips with
ranunculus

IT'S PERFECTLY ALRIGHT TO PLACE FLOWERS GIVEN UPON A GUEST'S ARRIVAL IN A BUCKET OR SINK OF WATER TO ARRANGE LATER.

the bar

think of your bar as the watercooler conversation station of your party: it's an inviting place where guests mix their own cocktails and linger with other guests while you hobnob, too.

delicious drinks, then, are imperative. while most people will stick to easy classics, inspire them to escape the ordinary by placing lesser-known recipes on folded place cards, in frames or on the wall just above the mixing station.

take things one step further by creating a signature cocktail for your event. over the holidays we might serve a poinsettia—champagne, cointreau, cranberry juice—or an oopsie daisy—mint, pear and lime juices, vodka—on a hot summer afternoon.[4]

take stock

THE TRAY:
- ▶ 2 clear spirits (vodka, gin)
- ▶ 2 brown spirits (rum, bourbon)
- ▶ 1 red wine
- ▶ 1 white wine
- ▶ 1 club soda
- ▶ 1 champagne
- ▶ 1 nonalcoholic drink that guests can personalize
(mix 1 liter seltzer, the juice of 1 large lime, 1 large sliced and muddled cucumber, ½ tsp sea salt)

- ▶ 1 bottle opener/corkscrew
- ▶ 1 small ice bucket with tongs
- ▶ 1 pretty bowl of precut wedges and rounds of lemons, limes and oranges
- ▶ 8 coasters
- ▶ all-purpose lowball and highball glasses (for wine and drinks on the rocks. or, use acrylic.)
- ▶ old-fashioned coupes (for bubbly and drinks served "up")

how to shake a cocktail

1
pour ingredients into a tin shaker that is ⅞ full of ice and cover with a glass, pressing down to seal.

2
holding the tin tight at the rim to help keep the cocktail cool, shake the tin hard and fast over your shoulder—like you're shaking a present to figure out what's inside.

3
once the tin looks frosty, strain the ingredients into a glass.

shaken or stirred?

SHAKE:
cocktails that combine spirits with other, full-bodied ingredients (e.g., juice, milk, cream liqueurs, simple syrup, sour mix or egg whites). the movement aerates the mixers into a delightfully frothy, wonderfully cloudy consistency. mai tais, white russians and margaritas are shaken.

STIR:
cocktails that are strictly spirit-based or use very light mixers such as manhattans, negronis, and—yes, mr. bond—martinis.

fill lowball glasses with
a single jumbo ice cube
made in a muffin tin.
if you're so inclined, fill
the tray halfway with
water, freeze, then pop
a lemon round, a heart-
shaped strawberry sliver
or a mint leaf atop each
cube, top with more water
and freeze. use boiled
filtered water to make
them crystal clear.

THE CART:
a room-changing piece that also works as a coffee
trolley, plant stand, breakfast-in-bed server, and poolside
towel and lemonade holder.

stock it with the contents of the tray plus:
▶ 1 cocktail shaker with strainer attachment
▶ 1 stirring spoon
▶ cocktail picks
▶ cocktail umbrellas and/or swizzle sticks
▶ muddler (for crushing limes and mint. the end
of a wooden spoon works just fine, too.)
▶ cutting board
▶ paring knife
▶ 2-sided measure (a "jigger")
▶ decanters
▶ pint or pilsner beer glasses
▶ selection of workhorse and specialty mixers (vermouth,
aperol, lillet, angostura bitters, simple syrup[5])
▶ jar of luxardo maraschino cherries
▶ stack of cocktail napkins[6]
▶ a little personality piece—we love 1950s-era critters in
lucite by brazilian artist abraham palatnik, in wood by
alexander girard and in bronze by walter bosse

THE COUNTER:
(e.g.: a credenza countertop, kitchen island, dining room
table or sideboard)

stock it with the contents of the cart plus:
▶ 1 hourglass beverage glass jar or vintage ceramic crock
to dispense a punch or signature cocktail
▶ 1 similar dispenser for your nonalcoholic beverage or
water with lemon and cucumber

[4] if inspiration fails to strike, give a classic recipe a twist and rename it something
utterly fantastical like we did with the oopsie daisy. it'll become one of the things
people talk about the morning after. (hopefully, fondly.)
[5] so long as you're not embarking on a night of sweet drinks, caster (superfine) sugar
in lieu of simple syrup works just fine.
[6] why not have paper napkins monogrammed in an exquisite font with gold foil?
or linen ones embroidered in lipstick red?

“the party's w you are.

here

GEORGIA LORRISON
the bad and the beautiful

the table

treat your cupboards as a dressing-up closet: collect trays and bowls in a particular theme (brass, silver, ceramic) or color so you can mix, match and repurpose them on a whim. amass a hodgepodge of old silver. mix modern finds with grandma's cut glass. vintage coupes in clear or lightly tinted glass easily become condiment holders and dessert plates. cake stands in varying heights create visual interest and instantly make even the plainest flour biscuit look delightful; they can also be turned upside-down and used for crudité (along the ring) and dip (place a bowl in the hollow pedestal).

if space is tight, host a buffet or cocktail party instead of a seated dinner. if you're set on a proper meal, seat guests on pretty floor cushions around the coffee table and serve foods that don't need to be cut.

darling

"I MEAN, IN WHAT WORLD DO YOU HAVE THIRTY OF ANYTHING?" *sarah sophie flicker*

lay it on the table

▸ roll out a length of lining paper across the table under the plates and secure it at both ends underneath with tape. then write out the seating plan with chunky black markers.

▸ cloth napkins[7] atop a bare table says chicly casual.

▸ spell out a word (or the name of the guest of honor) in carnations or roses. pick up the styrofoam letters from the craft store or flower market.

▸ coat individual glass water bottles with spray adhesive and roll them in glitter; set one at each place setting for a party favor they'll savor on the ride home or the morning after.

▸ use old album covers in complementary hues as placemats.

▸ fill apothecary jars with folded bits of beautiful paper for an after-dinner game.

▸ cluster vibrant bottles of italian or mexican sodas on a silver tray.

play your (place)cards right

▸ fancy paper cards inscribed with your guests' informal nicknames or terms of endearment

▸ during the holidays, a paper gift tag tied around a glittery ornament

▸ mini baguettes of bread in flat paper bags, with names (and the menu) written on top

▸ scrabble tiles placed on the wooden stands straight from the game box

▸ granny smith apples written on in white, black or metallic paint pens

▸ paper flags tucked horizontally into the tops of uncracked walnut shells

▸ giant letter initials

if you forget which side your bread plate and water should go on, discreetly make an "a-ok" sign with each hand, under the table. the "b" on your left is for bread. the "d" on your right is for drink.

---

[7] stylist martha ward keeps hers—monogrammed french linen "the size of pillowcases"—crisp and bright by washing them in the australian diaper detergent napisan. (for spills, she says, soak them overnight, dry and then iron.)

the music

think of your party like a film. there's a plot (your theme), a cast of characters (your guest list), meet-cutes[8] and twists in the storyline. what's your soundtrack?

create your own...

▸ match the music to the mood you want to create.

▸ make it three to four hours long (enough time to forget the first song before it repeats).

▸ avoid clichéd, overplayed songs. (that being said, toss one in just for fun.)

▸ juxtapose old with new.

▸ stick to complementary genres—pop and billie holiday, for instance, don't mix. strangely, french rap and billie holiday do.

▸ think regionally. "i like to use a latin compilation," says dj and entrepreneur hannah bronfman. "great background music that gets people in the mood but won't have them trying to listen to which individual song is playing while they're in conversation."

▸ match the tempo to the occasion. a cocktail party or pre-dinner playlist calls for an upbeat vibe to match the energy of the group chatter; mellow, down-tempo songs are better suited for late-night mixes.

▸ avoid sending messages. while it may be tempting to play overt love songs during a romantic dinner-for-two, limit yourself to one.

▸ use a digital player (iTunes, spotify, soundcloud) to craft playlists for different parts of the event or times of day. create an all-purpose mix (not too loud, fast or slow) that you can turn to on a whim.

*

all-occasion musicians

• django reinhardt
• nina simone
• françoise hardy
• miles davis
• feist
• stan getz

---

[8] meet-cute: that moment in a film or television script when a future romantic couple meet for the first time, and in an unlikely, zany, must-have-been-destiny (aka: cute) way.

"call me" blondie

"nothing but flowers"
the talking heads

"baby did a bad,
bad thing"
chris isaak

"please mr. postman"
the marvelettes

"some velvet morning"
primal scream

"7 heure du mat"
jacqueline tai eb

"damn girl"
justin timberlake

"be my baby"
the ronettes

"you really got me"
the kinks

"raspberry beret"
prince

...or cheat

professionally curated and paced, film soundtracks set
a clear mood and add a natural rise-and-fall to the pulse
of the party. these twelve in particular are tailor-made
for late-night cocktail parties, sunday afternoon get-
togethers or quiet dinners at home.

▶ *buena vista social club:* high-energy and authentically
hip cuban music.
▶ *the big chill:* soulful 1960s motown at its finest.
▶ *pulp fiction:* a goldmine of random, long-lost gems.
▶ *city of god:* original scores along with favorites from
1970s brazil.
▶ *a man and a woman:* romantic french tunes as light
and fluffy as a croissant.
▶ *almost famous:* a perfectly mixed album of 1970s stars
from elton john to lynyrd skynyrd.
▶ *lost in translation:* airy, moody background music with
euro flair.
▶ *the harder they come:* reggae without the cliché from
jimmy cliff, toots and the maytals and desmond dekker.
▶ *american graffiti:* forty-one early rock 'n' roll and
doo-wop wonders.
▶ *pretty in pink:* the most romantic new wave mashup
ever, complete with echo and the bunnymen, new order
and the smiths.
▶ *the royal tenenbaums:* a multigenerational mélange—
the clash and elliott smith; paul simon and bob dylan.

what's your favorite p

dress, heels and a cock

not turning up. best

by pharrell williams

the studio 54 era

a dash of lipstick, a sp

in front of the mi

i'm a champagne gi

after a party? *tax*

[pa]rty outfit? *a fabulous* [cockt]ail ring. party no-no? [*bad*] dance song? *"happy"* [*or*] *anything disco from* [p]re-party ritual? [*a sp*]*ritz of perfume, a twirl* [*in the mirr*]*or.* party cocktail? [*champagne*]*.* favorite way home [*a cab*,] *please!* DEBORAH LLOYD, *our chief creative officer*

curating the guest list

one fundamental factor that makes new york city such a vibrant, lively and interesting city is the mix of people who live in it. everyone has wildly different backgrounds and different futures, yet cross at their particular mutual interests. or coffee shops.

the same is said of a party and its guests. of course there are times when nothing sounds better than brunch with college friends, but in the grand scope of *soirée* generalizations, it makes for a much more interesting event when you cross-pollinate.

don't overthink it. just ask yourself:

"who's interesting?"
these will be your creative firebirds, originals, amazing dressers, elegant thinkers, subversives and excellent friends. these are the people who inspire you, whoever they may be.

and then, from that group,

"who will appreciate the party?"
when alexa hirschfeld and her brother james, cofounders of the digital and paper card company paperless post, threw an electronic dance party one february "on a random midwinter night, in a brooklyn warehouse, it was important to invite the slice of our friends who'd have fun in that type of environment. people who would dress up, dance till dawn and take lots of pictures," says alexa. "this is not the same crowd i'd invite to my wedding." nor, necessarily, to her thirtieth birthday party, which was an intimate dinner at her parents' house. for that, the guest list—a mix of old and new friends—"needed to be a reflection of me at that moment. but at the same time, i thought about if they would be at my thirty-fifth and my fortieth birthday parties, too."

1
be naturally nosy.

2
their pets, their children and, if part of a couple, how they met their partner are three universal topics.

3
if you're in a group of friends, play an innocuous but telling question game. ("what do you eat in your pajamas when no one's looking?")

4
be a good listener.

5
think on your feet so you can play off what the other person says.

6
don't be so formal. (see point number 1.)

✳ ARE YOU A PARTY GOER, THROWER OR AVOIDER? "ALL THREE." *iris apfel*

if we could invite anyone past, present, real or fictional
to dinner[9] (and were forced to keep that list under
thirty), these characters would snag an invitation:

jackie kennedy

john f. kennedy

sarah silverman

mr. darcy

gloria steinem

liz meriwether

miss piggy

holly golightly

iris apfel

jimmy fallon

cecilia dean

bell hooks

lucille ball

lauren bacall

james bond

lena dunham

truman capote

diana vreeland

miranda july

carrie bradshaw

paul newman

dominique levy

nicki minaj

shirley maclaine

oprah winfrey

[9] this, by the way, is a very fun party game to play.

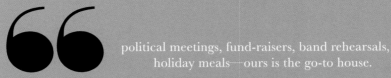

political meetings, fund-raisers, band rehearsals,
holiday meals—ours is the go-to house.

i like throwing a whole bunch
of people together and
seeing what happens.

people are curious; they want to be exposed to interesting ideas,
and while no one likes to be lectured to,
i find that they do want to help and understand each other.

so whatever the cause, i figure out how
to give people an action.

because then they'll be excited to get on board
and be part of the solution. and i give them information:
i'm passionate about certain topics but because
i'm learning as i go, i don't put myself in charge
of that because there are other people
who can give a nuanced perspective.
i find that organizations[10] are eager to send someone
to speak, even at a small gathering. so

i'll book a great speaker
to say some words.

short, sweet and couched in a lot of fun.
i'll put out some wine and cheese and drinks for the people who don't drink—
people always migrate to the kitchen, so we've given up that fight
and just put all the food in there—and then try to have an activity.

[10] on a recent trip to washington, d.c., sarah discovered that activist organizations are open to
wacky ideas. "they are used to a lot of politicians and policymakers coming through the doors,"
she says. "but they also want creative people to make advocating for justice a cool thing."

i like to add some theatrics and music.

to present things in a beautiful, humanist, nondivisive way,
like song nights with a hilarious emcee, topical charades or a fashion-y raffle.
everything can't always be treated as a party, but if it can be, it should be!

i trust my guests.

i trust them to put food on their plate, make themselves a drink,
figure out who to sit next to. but if i see someone struggling,
i introduce her to someone or, better yet, give her a job—
opening wine, telling people where to put their coats.
tasks force people to interact and that leads to conversations.

the more casual you can make an event, the better,

whether you hold it at your own house or offsite at a restaurant or club.
i don't do anything that feels upstairs-y, downstairs-y. that's fun-prohibitive.
the invitation states six to eight, or seven to nine, but people end up staying.
bands play. people sing. the twenty-somethings will help clean up.
the drunk people deejay. in fact, we usually have every generation represented,
from people in their seventies down to my one-year-old.
at a certain point, age stops mattering, right?

everyone just gives each other a different perspective.

SARAH SOPHIE FLICKER
*sarah is a brooklyn-based writer, director and founder
of political cabaret group the citizen's band*

My thirtieth birthday dinner was really small and intimate, but I sent out my invitation by e-mail. It still conveyed that my mom was cooking oyster pie and we'd be having cake in my living room.

ALEXA HIRSCHFELD,
cofounder, paperless post

When I got married I designed and typeset the invitations myself. The RSVPs all came back with handwritten corrections about spacing and layout—most of my friends are graphic designers! I loved them so much I had them framed.

DEBORAH CAMPLIN, *our svp of design*

I once got a hand-delivered posy, simply labeled with 'pour mémoire' and the date of the event.

MARTHA WARD, *stylist*

invitations

quite often a simple text or phone call will do, but there's something so joyous about getting a little envelope in the post or a beautiful digital card among all the junk mail in your inbox.

why not... scribble a personal note and the details on a postcard? tuck your invitation into pristine vintage metal cigarette holders and hand-deliver them? write out addresses with a black sharpie for an artful, casual feel? give each one a little spritz of your favorite perfume? (just one spritz!) inject them with a little cultural know-how: if you're throwing a fondue party, include the (rather humorous) rules of the tradition. add a touch of gold foil? press the envelope closed with a wax seal?

useful phrases:
use **FOR YOUR LOVELY EYES ONLY** if the party is a private one, or a surprise.

play with grammar and write **DRESS: UP!** under the pertinent details ("date:" "time:" "location:") to encourage guests to arrive looking a little fancy.

S

mrs. lilien

the title character of virginia woolf's mrs. dalloway—*the grand dame londoner clarissa—is known for her bond street parties. ("everything for the party," as woolf wrote.) the california-based graphic designer and blogger* mrs. lilien—*first name kelley—approaches her festivities with an air of devil-may-care glamour. this is a glimpse into their pre-party preparations.*

mrs. dalloway

"oh it was a letter from her! this blue envelope; that was her hand. and he would have to read it."

"her only gift was knowing people almost by instinct, she thought, walking on. if you put her in a room with someone, up went her back like a cat's; or she purred."

"faint sounds rose in spirals up the well of the stairs; the swish of a mop; tapping; knocking; a loudness when the front door opened; a voice repeating a message in the basement; the chink of silver on a tray; clean silver for the party."

"it made no difference at this hour of the night to mrs. walker among the plates, saucepans, cullenders, frying-pans, chicken in aspic, ice-cream freezers, pared crusts of bread, lemons, soup tureens and pudding basins which, however hard they washed up in the scullery seemed to be all on top of her, on the kitchen table, on chairs, while the fire blared and roared, the electric lights glared, and still supper had to be laid. all she felt was, one prime minister more or less made not a scrap of difference to mrs. walker."

mrs. lilien

"digital or paper depends on my mood. it's not beyond
the norm to search out high-resolution gold sequins on
google image, or an old illustration of carmen miranda
for a patio party. for one spring dinner, the paper invitation was so thick you wanted to rub it on your face.
it was so velvety."

"i love an intimate, super-special, ceremonial gathering
of people. then i invite a wild card. if there's ever a lull,
i turn to that person. it keeps everyone on their toes."

"i have a whole buffet filled with bits and bobs, and it's
ritualistic: the taking out, the putting away. i get excited
about the little things. i searched for weeks to find
vintage plastic playboy club swizzle sticks. sometimes
one at a time. people might brag, 'i have china service
for twelve.' well, i have swizzle sticks for sixty."

"the morning of, i wake up and think 'oh shit.' there's
either a mess i made from last night's prep work or a
new mess from one of the kids. everyone should have an
'oh shit' cupboard or closet where they shove random
things before the party."

"one christmas day dinner, i ordered tamales, enchi-
ladas, chips and salsas from this delicious but dodgy
mexican place. i picked it up on christmas eve and it
sat in the refrigerator in aluminum trays overnight. then
i served it all on my best china. i also put a shot glass
at each place setting and filled them with really good
tequila. we went around the table, and each guest—we
always host the 'orphans'—had to stand up, reflect and
say what they're grateful for. people cry, people laugh."

DÉCOR "and lucy, coming into the drawing-room with her tray held out, put the giant candlesticks on the mantelpiece, the silver casket in the middle, turned the crystal dolphin towards the clock."

HER OUTFIT "clarissa, plunging her hand into the softness, gently detached the green dress and carried it to the window... by artificial light the green shone, but lost its colour now in the sun. she would mend it. her maids had too much to do. she would wear it to-night. she would take her silks, her scissors, her—what was it?—her thimble, of course, down into the drawing-room, for she must also write, and see that things generally were more or less in order."

LIGHTING "and, she murmured, as the night grew later, as people went, one found old friends; quiet nooks and corners; and the loveliest views...just a few fairy lamps, clarissa dalloway had said, in the back garden! but she was a magician! it was a park."

ESCAPING THE ORDINARY "every time she gave a party she had this feeling of being something not herself, and that everyone was unreal in one way; much more real in another."

"years ago, for halloween, i adhered giant wired-felt
bats to this long wall in the dining room, and when
i took them off, off came patches of paint. so instead
of repainting the wall, i redecorate it every new holiday—paper honeycomb balls, from eighteen inches
to five inches, opened halfway and cascading from the
corner of the ceiling like a snowdrift in winter; this fall,
i pinned leaves gathered from the neighborhood."

"on the table i do place cards using my daughter's toys
as holders. then i write messages on the backs for the
other guests to see, like 'just smile and nod' or 'please
pass the vodka.'"

"at home, no shoes and an a-line shift. usually clip-on
earrings—ones that fall off five, six times. maybe into
someone's drink. a vibrant lip, always. and a tiny spot
of glitter somewhere in my eye makeup. it takes not
more than ten minutes."

"i light up my house like a shrine. uplighting—white
canisters on a tilt—creates interesting shadows. lanterns
both hanging and on the floor. flameless, flickering
candles that are battery-operated and i can set to go
at a certain time. i definitely don't have an aversion to
stringing lights across the table."

"my favorite take on things is mostly nice with a little
bit of naughty. pompous but playful. i love looking at
the party pictures in *vanity fair* filled with swanky people
with three last names. then i think, 'how amazing would
it be if they all had paper masks on sticks?'"

all-ages entertaining

joy cho, mom to four-year-old ruby and one-year-old coco, and voice of the blog *oh joy!*, reminds us that there are so many better ways to spend an afternoon than hovering around a semi-stranger's living room with nothing more than a chicken nugget and a sip of fruit juice in your belly.

adult-friendly kid parties

if your child's social circle has yet to hit the five-year mark, expect parents to stay and act as extra chaperones.[11]

TIME: ten thirty, no later than eleven, in the morning. "that leaves enough time for the kids to play a bit, and everyone to have lunch, before naptime at one o'clock."

LOCATION: a city park, the back room of a pizzeria, even the beloved neighborhood restaurant that doesn't get busy 'til evening. while tot-size festivities are under way, you want to give your grown-up guests access to adult-size seating, the opportunity to order an adult drink and the freedom to subtly come and go if needed. at an offsite you can't get too elaborate: you'll have an hour or less to set up, which encourages you to be thoughtful, yet relaxed, about whatever you have planned.

SNACKS: a festive version of a child's normal lunch: almond butter and jelly sandwiches cut into stars and potato skins topped with broccoli and cauliflower

it's play time

• set up a colorful backdrop and a dress-up station off to the side complete with sunglasses, top hats and other fun props. let the kids take turns having their photos taken.

• put out enough paint, mini easels and canvases for everyone—or prop life-sized ones on the grass—and let the kids create their own paintings to take home. (don't forget the mini aprons.)

• better yet, crack open the tops of eggs and empty/wash them, fill with paint, and let the kids toss them at their canvases to create their own jackson pollock–like masterpieces.

• start with a decorate-your-own-apron station, then pour frosting into condiment squeeze jars to decorate cookies.

• enlist an artsy friend to paint faces.

• turn a backyard or park area into a low-fi carnival with game stations (ball toss using large metal pails, bobbing for apples).

[11] ages six to nine, parents should include specifics in the invitation, whether it's "grown-ups welcome!", or, conversely, "a couple of hours off is our gift to you." at celebrations for ten-year-olds and up, you can assume the event is only for the birthday girl's/boy's friends.

florets. or food on sticks: raspberries, cheddar cubes, mozzarella balls and adorable mouse melons (also known as mexican gherkins) are just a handful of things cho has threaded onto skewers. "kids don't see it as a salad, they see it as something fun to eat." whether you're making your own picnic fare or ordering pizza by the slice, ensure there's a balance of healthy foods and special occasion sweets. "i make sure everything's not fried or based in cheese or bread and sneak some veggies and protein somewhere into the menu," she says.

GIFTS! give clear directions on the invitation. "if you've invited the entire preschool class that could mean thirty kids show up, and no child needs thirty presents, especially on one day," joy says. on invitations to her own daughters' parties, she's requested that guests donate to a charity in lieu of a gift or suggested they give books, which are compact (and noise-free!) for the parents, educational for the child and budget-friendly for the guest.

kid-friendly adult parties

ready your space with a little extra childproofing: move any breakables up high, shut the doors to any private rooms (like a home office, master bedroom or nursery), lock away toys that are overly complicated or have tiny parts but leave out toys that are good for groups of kids of varying ages. "so no glitter glue or legos," joy says, "but yes to the mini kitchen with the pretend food."

if you're expecting a lot of kids, consider hiring a sitter.

ask little helpers to set out utensils, put pita chips into a bowl or adhere stickers to plain place cards. older ones can string twinkle lights, place drinks in ice or make a digital playlist. "it helps them take some ownership of the party and to feel really proud when their friends—big and small—arrive," joy enthuses.

have two sizes of seating. "i rent kid-size tables and chairs that are more comfortable—and cuter." similarly, keep elements of the food to their scale. "either gourmet versions of kid food or," she notes, "kid-size portions of adult food."

make time for a fun-for-the-whole-family activity. joy swears by anything involving decorating—like building gingerbread houses or dyeing easter eggs (a great moment for photos). if the party isn't quite ready to wind down at the end of the night or a boisterous crowd of friends arrive late, corral all the kids in one room and pop in a G-rated movie with widespread appeal: *mary poppins* (1964), *freaky friday* (1976), *the muppets take manhattan* (1984), *babe* (1995) or *ratatouille* (2007).

an all-ages menu
"i always focus on the food and beverages, no matter what the ages," joy, who details these recipes on her blog, says.

▸ turkey meatloaf-stuffed pumpkins, using softball-sized gourds
▸ mini spinach-dip bread bowls
▸ egg in the basket with sourdough bread, slices of avocado and a side of sriracha for the over-eighteen set
▸ pizza pot pie stuffed with baby bella mushrooms, shallots and arrabbiata sauce
▸ peach pie milkshakes with artisanal honey-cinnamon ice cream, fresh peaches and nutmeg
▸ cardamom & cream cheese squares with a vanilla wafer crust, fresh nutmeg and maple syrup

catnip for kids:

- electronic gaming systems
- acoustic guitars
- heirloom chess sets

✳

joy does throw strictly adults-only soirees, too. for her husband's thirty-fifth birthday, she scribbled "hooray! adults' night out!" at the bottom of the invitation as a not-so-subtle hint to hire a sitter.

mi casa es tu casa.
(almost.)

the no-brainer[12] houseguest breakfast kit
▶ a dark tea
▶ a great coffee
▶ a hearty doorstop of a loaf of bread from your local bakery, a good-quality butter and jam
▶ smoked salmon and cucumber slices
▶ a breakfast trifle (organic yogurt, berries, yogurt, berries, yogurt, almonds)

it's ok to say make it yourself.
a pour-your-own bar, a fix-your-own sandwich station and make-your-own coffee station helps guests feel at home and takes the pressure off of you to be a twenty-four-hour hostess.

there are two ways to treat an under-the-weather guest.
chicken soup or a hot toddy. to make a hot toddy: brew a cup of hot herbal tea. add 1 tsp honey and 1 small shot whiskey or bourbon. (limit one.)

[12] remember to ask about your guests' preferences. you can easily substitute in gluten-free bread, non-dairy milk or yogurt, herbal tea and granola for a nut allergy.

"be daring, be different, be impractical; be anything that will assert integrity of purpose and imaginative vision against the play-it-safers."

CECIL BEATON

the art of serving takeout on fine china

twists aren't just for cocktail garnishes.[13] a clever departure from the norm is always a lovely idea when you're entertaining. we think takeout, for instance, tastes better on fine china. the "ding!" of the front doorbell during the clink of early evening cocktails and the parade of crisp white plastic bags into the kitchen[14] is a ceremonious move that surprises guests, alludes to a refreshingly devil-may-care attitude on your part and elicits sparkling conversation.

[13] if new yorkers treat the city like their living room, then restaurants are their dining rooms. we take inspiration from elsie de wolfe, the actress and interior decorator also credited with inventing the concept of the cocktail party, who threw a celebration dinner at a coin-operated automat in midtown. she covered the restaurant's tables with her own linens, china and silver; the guests picked their own entrees.
[14] dishes served family-style—curries, salads, tagines, dumplings, pizza, pastas—work best.

the trick is to invert expectations: combine two things that aren't intended to go together; pair one really fancy thing with one more common.

it was on the ceremonial stroke of midnight at the lavish and carefully orchestrated black and white ball that truman capote served a buffet of quite everyday food: chicken hash, spaghetti with meatballs, scrambled eggs and sausages. it's since been called the "party of the century."

a little thoughtful whimsy goes a long way.

other whimsical juxtapositions

▶ bake and serve individual shepherd's pie (or chocolate cake) in ovenproof ceramic mugs.
▶ teacups and saucers as soup bowls
▶ vintage ashtrays as dual soy sauce dishes and chopstick rests for sushi takeout
▶ a tall china coffeepot for pouring out a round of martinis as you circle the room
▶ unveil game night essentials (cards, dice, chips) in a jewelry box.
▶ serve sides in clear, lidded candy jars at an outdoor buffet.
▶ mini food-safe paint pails to serve condiments, with pastry brushes for spreading them
▶ "hello my name is" stickers adhered back-to-back on toothpicks to identify cheese
▶ souvenir spoons as fancy jam and sauce servers
▶ use silver julep cups as festive serving containers for cheese straws. (line each cup with a linen napkin to prevent salt and oils from coming in contact with the silver.)
▶ heavy crystal goblets for individual portions of comfort foods: mashed potatoes, seven-layer dip (salsa, guacamole, cheese, black olives)
▶ serve gastropub fish and chips at home in their large family-style paper box, atop a white linen tablecloth with formal silverware, red wine in proper glasses and a side of freshly cut lemon halves.

a really
strong
really dim
really, really
the house

drink.
lights.
tasty food.
smelling
really good.*

*do less, and do it abundantly.

who would have thought

create inspired menus by serving an item in the left column with something unexpectedly delicious-sounding in the right.

casual + fancy

casual	fancy
burgers	champagne
corn on the cob	burgundy
grilled cheese sandwiches	toasted brioche rounds, crème fraiche, caviar
mac & cheese	oysters
fried chicken	petit filet mignons
egg rolls or spring rolls	soufflé
pimento cheese on celery	lobster salad with endives
beer	baked camembert
chili	crunchy asparagus with mayonnaise
deviled eggs	mesclun with champagne vinaigrette
french fries	prosciutto-wrapped figs with mozzarella
tacos	antipasto of meats, cheeses, vegetables & bruschetta
dumplings	pâté & water crackers or crusty bread
soft pretzels	mini gratins
spaghetti & meatballs	crudité & aioli
omelettes	duck confit
popcorn	minty peas
guacamole & chips	consommé
shepherd's pie	radishes, butter & fleur de sel
clam chowder	thyme gougères
tuna salads	cornichons
paella	beef bourguignon
hashbrowns	eggs in pots (oeufs en cocotte)
potato salad	caramelized onion tartlets
bbq ribs	smoked mussels
submarine sandwiches	salmon & watercress salad
s'mores	fondue
black and white cookies	sushi rolls
brownies	tiramisu
donuts	chocolate babka
banana pudding	strawberries romanoff
hot fudge sundaes	macarons
_____	_____
_____	_____
_____	_____
_____	_____

(did we forget something?)

47

fun and games

there comes a point in every festivity that one of the following will suddenly sound very appealing:

▶ poker
▶ pictionary
▶ scrabble
▶ hearts
▶ champong (beer pong, with cups of champagne)
▶ apples to apples (rated PG)
▶ cards against humanity (rated R)
▶ white elephant gift exchange (with leftovers, party decorations and/or one-of-a-kind party favors as "gifts")

running charades

TO PLAY: divide guests into two teams and appoint a single clue-giver to keep score. (that person is switzerland.) each team writes a list of twenty of the following: memorable movies, books, songs, tv shows and names of well-known people and discreetly gives their list to the clue-giver, who is positioned equidistant between the two teams. (at least ten feet, to keep things lively.) team a's written list becomes team b's clue list and vice versa. so, shhh.

the game starts when each team sends a player running to the clue-giver for the first item on their (new) list to act out for the team. the teammate who guesses correctly runs full steam to retrieve the next clue to act out, and so on. first team to reach the end of their list wins!

break the ice
a game of ten questions:

• women should always...

• men should always...

• there's a time and a place for...

• first thing in the morning...

• last thing at night...

• the movie of my life would star...

• the soundtrack to it would feature...

• my mom...

• happiness is...

• my greatest love is...

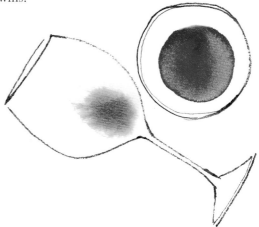

a wine tasting with a twist

BEFORE THE PARTY: pick up a selection of wines (between four and eight) from different regions at your local wine shop. if the wine shop has any fun facts about your choices, gather them at this time. once home, write a little monologue for each wine, as if the wine were a person and introducing itself to the group. (*where is it from? what does it taste like? what is its background? what does it like? what does it not like?* anything except its actual name.)

disguise each bottle so any distinctive labeling is hidden (spray them with adhesive and roll each in a different color of glitter; place each in a distinctive paper gift bag; cover each in wrapping paper from the neck down—be sure to keep track).

AT THE PARTY: set out the wines and wineglasses. read each monologue aloud for your guests (regional accents optional) and then give them a copy of the descriptions on paper.

THEIR TASK: taste and match!

sticky foreheads

TO PLAY: privately write the name of a famous person or character (past, present, real or fictional) on a sticky note for each guest. making sure that each player doesn't see the one they're getting, stick the note to their forehead. once everyone is named, each player asks the group questions that can be answered by "yes," "no" and "not applicable" to try and figure out who they are. ("am i a woman?" "am i in history books?" "am i real?" and so forth.)

 the fictional tenenbaum family in wes anderson's 2001 film *the royal tenenbaums* has a dedicated games closet filled floor to ceiling with games both local and international. a green monopoly house punctuates the light's pull chain.

"a photographer went to a socialite party in new york. as he entered the front door, the host said, *'i love your pictures—they're wonderful. you must have a fantastic camera.'* he said nothing until dinner was finished, then: *'that was a wonderful dinner. you must have a terrific stove.'*"

SAM HASKINS

documenting the party

"if you didn't take the picture, you weren't there," **GARRY WINOGRAND** once aptly noted. here are some people who famously were:

TOD PAPAGEORGE. his lo-fi lens into studio 54 from 1978–80 immortalized an organic, glittering decadence in manhattan. **TOM PALUMBO.** he's better known for his photographs for *vogue* and *harper's bazaar,* but his snapshots of intimate dinners around les halles, paris, in the 1960s feel like modern-day film stills. **PATRICK MCMULLAN.** he kept a photographic diary of 1980s new york nightlife that shook uptown glamour and downtown eccentricity into a potent visual cocktail.

while this was before the age of iPhones, their photos weren't taken with fancy cameras. what they had was a bold curiosity and a sophisticated way with snapshots. so we imagine that if garry (one of the greatest photographers of the twentieth century, who focused mainly on documenting new york city life) had an instagram account today, his unfiltered, off-kilter, invasive and quite often humorous photographic observations would be well commented on.

visual mementos bring back the snippets of small talk, conversational eurekas and festive shenanigans for those who were there. those who weren't can fill in the blanks with their imagination.[15]

---

[15] "a picture is worth ten thousand words" is a chinese proverb that's quite apt here. though it's not a chinese proverb. its origins are in advertising. in 1921, street railway advertising company's national advertising manager, frederick r. barnard, took out an ad in advertising journal *printers ink* with the headline "one look is worth a thousand words." he did it again in 1927, switching "look" to "picture," "a thousand" to "ten thousand" and the source from ancient japanese to ancient chinese. he's later quoted as saying he attributed the quote to an asian proverb so the public would take it seriously. perhaps he was inspired by a line in ivan s. turgenev's 1862 novel *fathers and sons.* ("the drawing shows me at one glance what might be spread over ten pages in a book.")

---

how to take a great photo

from one of our favorite nyc-based photography duos and collaborators daemian smith and christine suarez:

1

pay attention to light. "this may seem obvious, but so many people overlook it. it sets the mood, gives shape to things and tells a big part of the picture's story."

2

move in close. "don't be shy about cozying up to your subject. focusing on the details will make the image more compelling."

3

play with angles. "instead of shooting straight on, try taking two steps to the left or right, or snapping from a lower angle."

4

the great photo may happen when you're not planning it. "sometimes the candid shots have the most power."

5

take more photos than you think you need.

celebrate everyday social occasions.

one of the pieces at the sotheby's auction for brooke
astor's estate in 2012 was a worn, dog-eared leather-
bound guest book. mrs. astor kept it in the entryway
at ferncliff, the family estate near rhinebeck, new york.
cover to cover this particular edition chronicled every
guest who ever dropped by, from 1924–1960. while
some merely signed it, more wrote notes that extended
into p.p.s.'s and doodled elaborate illustrations.
similarly, a friend of a friend snaps a mini polaroid
of everyone who walks through her door—from best
friends to the electrician—and hangs them in a progres-
sive grid formation on the wall above her fireplace.

along with the actual parties.

take everyone's photo as soon as they arrive. have
a stash of props to grab from—glitter cat-eye glasses,
crowns, paper handlebar moustaches and red lips on
sticks, paper bag masks,[16] photographic faces of iconic
people with elastic backs or on sticks[17]—or drop an
out-of-the-ordinary scenic "backdrop" (blow up a
photographic scene on wall-size poster paper or hang
streamers vertically) for people to stand against.
a little silliness is an instant icebreaker.

---

[16] in the 1950s, *new yorker* cartoonist saul steinberg began whimsically drawing simple
and artful faces on paper bags. over the next decade, his friend, photographer inge
morath, took a series of thoughtful portraits of him and his friends wearing them in
social settings.
[17] "i was the first to photograph twiggy in the united states. she was an overnight
sensation. everyone wanted to be twiggy. i suggested everyone wear twiggy masks,
which were shot and manufactured in the studio a week before the shoot. i believe
we manufactured over five hundred masks of which i have a few left. we gave
them out to the crowds who gathered to watch the shoot at the selected locations.
although the participants promised to give the masks back, they mysteriously
disappeared." melvin sokolsky

*

goody bags

goody bags can be easily
dismissed as something
best confined to kids
parties and swag bags.
we care to differ.

it's a chance to share your
good taste with all those
you love. fill takeout boxes
with leftover dessert
or wrap flowers from
the table in pretty paper
or newspaper;
the polaroid you snapped
of your guest at the
beginning of the night,
or a CD of the party's
playlist is delightful, too.
just make sure you have
enough of the various
goodies to go around.

like mother, like daughter.

daisy de villeneuve

THE HOSTESS

the vibrant and original paris-based english illustrator and writer has put her signature—witty quips and punchy, felt-tipped marker drawings—on everything from issues of vogue *magazine and her own books to fashion textiles to oversized bib necklace placemats (inspired by our own) for a private kate spade new york dinner. she's jan's daughter.*

THERE'S SOMETHING ABOUT...

"my mom is traditional. proper silverware. everything matches. i don't know that she even plays music. but she always creates a really fun environment."

MY KIND OF PARTY

"i don't cook, so i tend to do a really great tea party."

& fantastically vice versa.

jan de villeneuve

---

the ohio-born model and actress graced the pages of british and italian vogue *throughout the late 1960s and early 1970s, photographed by the likes of norman parkinson, helmut newton, patrick demarchelier and guy bourdin. she continues to work from her home base, just southeast of london. she's mom to daisy.*

"daisy has lived in a lot of places, but they have one thing in common: minimal kitchens. she never seems to have a stove."

"a good example is daisy's twenty-first birthday. i cooked a june lunch for fifty people. it was one of those one o'clock lunches that lasts until dinner, with leftovers served at seven."

THE INVITATIONS "as part of the RSVP, i ask my guests what time i should expect them in order to stagger arrivals. some come for tea at four o'clock before dinner, others for wine after dinner. and everyone drinks early here, so i transition from cocktails to wine at about seven."

DÉCOR "i use a colorful tablecloth with mismatched plates, old english souvenir spoons, plastic forks in shocking pink and lots of candles. then i go to the flower market the day of the party and pick up pink roses and place them in a big yellow jug and serve the tea with royal memorabilia, like princess di and prince charles mugs.

my tea cosy makes guests laugh. it looks like a red knitted hat and is inscribed with two english expressions: 'more tea, vicar?'[18] and 'shall I be, mother?'"[19]

THE SOUNDTRACK "mostly 1970s and 1980s music, with some early hip-hop so people don't feel like they're at a disco—ZZ top, the eagles, alice cooper, run-D.M.C., tone lōc, dr. dre. i don't know any new hip-hop, by the way."

[18] a british phrase commonly associated with old sitcoms, wherein the lady of the house would announce "more tea, vicar?" in order to divert a naive vicar's attention from something uncouth unfolding. in real life, the phrase is used as an amusingly way to change the subject after a faux pas.
[19] the phrase means "shall i pour?" across the pond, where it's considered an honor to pour the tea.

"daisy made them after finding an old contact sheet of photos from her first birthday party. in them she's sitting in a bamboo high chair, eating cake and wearing a jump-suit from biba, one of my favorite london boutiques. it closed the year she was born. daisy just photocopied the contact sheet onto yellow paper.

the girls have made invitations since they were small— christmas, valentine's, birthday. it was economical plus it kept the girls busy on a sunday afternoon. i still get daisy to do the invitations and the place cards. she has really good handwriting."

"my mother was really good at socializing. she died last spring at ninety-six and was baking until the last min-ute. i've inherited things from her and my grandmother: old lace tablecloths, linen napkins, silver trays, these champagne coupes with hollow stems so you can see the bubbles float up.

i use the tablecloths all the time. i just put them in a pillowcase, knot it, tie a rubber band around the knot and throw into the hot wash.[20] i don't break the bank at the dry cleaners or worry when a guest spills wine. for dishes i use old spode china that looks like it's em-broidered with little red and blue bows. and a whole set of biba dishes that are more funky, brown and black with gold rims. for daisy's birthday, i put out some super-market lilies and daisies—huge bunches in big clear glass vases, so they looked like i gathered them in a field."

"the girls took care of the music. i checked on the salmon."

[20] jan gleaned this tip from a laundress to queen elizabeth.

"simple dishes from childhood: white bread, crusts cut off, buttered then covered in colorful sprinkles; toast made by heating the bread, using a cookie cutter to cut a heart or star in the middle and then frying an egg in the hole.

then i add some nice cheeses, ham, fine cupcakes, fruit dipped in white chocolate and my favorite tea— pg tips—plus some flavored varieties from mariage frères. my new trick is to buy boxed wine, then pour it into vintage glass carafes and throw the box away."

"at my mom's, the door is always open. not everybody will know each other, but will have made friends by the end of the evening. same with me. and people can always bring guests—as long as they aren't weirdos."

"i always start with a glass of bubbly. it's fizzy, pretty. daisy did the packaging for moët & chandon's rosé once, so for a while we had loads of pink champagne!

i like to serve food that tastes good, not just looks good on the plate. i've always had healthy, local foods in season. i raised my two daughters in sussex, near a farm, so our milk and eggs came from up the road. now i live in kent near the sea, so i pick up fresh, raw oysters for parties.

i love serving american things for english friends— pumpkin pie, the ham from *joy of cooking*. and english things for american friends—crumbles, puddings, custards. my summer pudding uses so many fresh raspberries and blueberries that the whole kitchen turns purple. for daisy's picnic, i made a big, foil-wrapped salmon with crème fraîche dressing, herbed pita with hummus and crudité, shrimp cocktail, big bowls of salad dressed with olive oil and lemon, boiled potatoes and green beans.

after dinner there's cheese and crackers, coffee and a big bowl of cherries, then my mother's famous strawberry-cream cake for dessert. it's angel food cake sliced into four layers, and interspersed with whipped cream that's flavored with pureed strawberries. seven layers total. then you ice the entire cake in that same pink cream."

"we both like handmade things and for people to feel comfortable—friendships, no fancy sauces, big fires in winter. the dishes and the food and the budget don't really matter as long as there's love and affection.

i hope i instilled in my daughter the same love for entertaining that my mom did in me."

parties in 5 days.

all during office hours.*
(aka: how to celebrate anything in a cubicle.)
*THIS ACTUALLY HAPPENED.

we love any excuse to celebrate, and no one on our team can resist the chance to toast the joyous occasions in our colleagues' lives.

what makes each one so special?

we believe entertaining is entertaining is entertaining, no matter where it happens. and so the way we throw a little soirée at work is just like how we throw them at home. (we highly encourage you to do the same.)

as at home, the details make the difference, so we enthusiastically tailor the food, decorations and music to the occasion's guest of honor, and we always make it a surprise. for a trio of moms-to-be, we wrote baby name ideas on little pieces of paper and attached them to the ends of balloon strings, compiled a menu with every one of their food cravings, and encouraged everyone to bring a children's book as a present. for a birthday girl who, all year, had been obsessed with guacamole, we turned a conference room into a full-on mexican fiesta (with guacamole).

no matter what the occasion, there are certain props that we find always come in handy more than the rest:

▶ real champagne glasses for a group toast
▶ stripey straws
▶ birthday candles (for everything!)
▶ conversation banners and gigantic letter balloons
▶ confetti
▶ a ringleader who sends out the secret e-vite and ensures everyone arrives
▶ lots of bite-sized confections

and we love that something always goes fantastically wrong—it gives us fodder to laugh about long after the party is over.

"wouldn't it be

amazin

if we spent as much energy

investing in

experi
enc

as we do investing in things?"

dream guests
are made of this

▶ come with a hearty appetite and a rested soul.
▶ don't show up early or, for a sit-down or time-sensitive event, arrive more than fifteen minutes late.
▶ arrive festively well dressed.[21]
▶ put your cell phone away.
▶ talk to the person on your left, and on your right. listen thoughtfully and ask questions.
▶ RSVP *tout de suite:* always respond to an invitation within three days.
▶ if you are suddenly unable to attend, give your hostess immediate notice.
▶ don't arrive at a loss for words. read the paper or a news website (you can't go wrong with *the new york times*).
▶ come armed with a few conversation starters...but don't feel compelled to channel oscar wilde.
▶ sit at the table at the same time as most of the other guests.
▶ pass dishes counterclockwise (to your right). unless everyone is already going left.
▶ ask if anyone would like the last piece before you take it.
▶ be the first to make a toast and the last to say good night.
▶ send a little thank-you gift,[22] either before or after.

[21] not in the mood? put on some bright lipstick, some clicking bangles and a pair of chic shoes with whatever you have on. that combination works anywhere, anytime, anyplace and turns frowns upside down, guaranteed.
[22] a heartfelt thank-you note or email the morning after. flowers that arrive an hour or two before the party starts. a bottle of champagne. a classic board game, a pint of ice cream from a nearby creamery. her favorite candle. the little film you shot during the event using your lo-fi hand-operated lomokino camera.

RUZWANA BAHIR

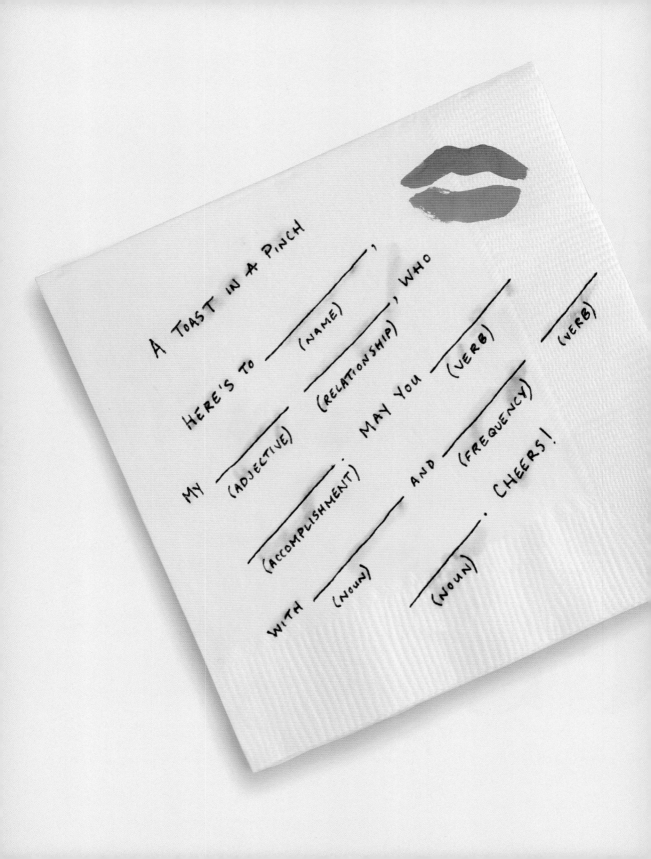

A TOAST IN A PINCH

HERE'S TO _____ (NAME), WHO

MY _____ (RELATIONSHIP) (ADJECTIVE). MAY YOU _____ (VERB)

_____ (ACCOMPLISHMENT) AND _____ (FREQUENCY) _____ (VERB)

WITH _____ (NOUN) _____ (NOUN). CHEERS!

the new traditions

"SERVE THE DINNER BACKWARD, DO ANYTHING—BUT FOR GOODNESS SAKE, DO SOMETHING WEIRD" *elsa maxwell*

the new york brunch

THE MOOD	relaxed weekend glamour
THE INVITATION	text, punctuated by one newspaper and egg skillet emoji
THE TABLE	a haphazard mix-and-match of stripes (plates), crystal (glasses) and florals (fresh)
THE DRINKS	strong coffee. mimosas. red snappers (*the signature drink at the st. regis hotel's king cole bar*)

    1 oz vodka
    2 oz tomato juice
    1 dash lemon juice
    2 dashes salt
    2 dashes black pepper
    2 dashes cayenne pepper
    3 dashes worcestershire sauce

    combine ingredients in cocktail shaker. shake vigorously. strain over ice and garnish with a lemon wedge.

THE MAIN DISHES	▸ fresh orange and grapefruit wedges ▸ skillet frittatas ▸ fluffy oven-fresh biscuits with turkey, arugula, swiss cheese, sweet and spicy mustard ▸ seasonal fruit compotes, cream, pats of butter, honey ▸ warm slices of chocolate babka (we frequently order from zabar's and russ & daughters)
THE PLAYLIST	"madeline" yo la tengo "sunny afternoon" the kinks "tous les garçons et les filles" françoise hardy "on the sunny side of the street" billie holiday "1234" feist
THE EXTRA SOMETHING	▸ take an after-brunch stroll around the neighborhood. ▸ send guests home with little brown paper sacks filled with tea towel–wrapped babka.

the shower

THE MOOD

somewhere between overtly feminine and positively frothy

THE INVITATION

traditional paper invitations that the guest of honor (and the best friends by her side) will want to have as keepsakes. include registry details and clearly note if it's a ladies-only or couples event.

THE MENU AND TABLE

offset a solid, sherbet-hued runner with a bricolage of patterned dessert plates and vintage teacups. (flea markets and estate sales are excellent resources.) then add:

▶ fruit tarts, petit fours and conversation heart sugar cookies ("baby cakes" for mom; "ever after" and "i do!" for the bride, written with icing markers) on cake stands
▶ enough crustless, triangular tea sandwiches—gouda and sun-dried tomato; curried chicken salad; salmon and cucumber—for three or four per guest, on antique vanity trays
▶ raspberries stuffed with a white or dark chocolate chip
▶ individual stacks of three macarons tied together with a ribbon

THE DRINKS

kir royale, ginger ale with a scoop of sorbet, exotic tea sachets fanned out on a pretty platter

THE PLAYLIST

kiss me, kiss me, kiss me the cure
beggars banquet the rolling stones
among my swan mazzy star

THE EXTRA SOMETHING

on the invitation, create a theme around the gifts. for the bride-to be, things she and her groom can share: monogrammed bed linens in a sophisticated neutral, with their initials entwined; a pair of mugs and china plates; a two-piece dessert set for celebratory homemade desserts. for the mom-to-be, a mix of precious cargo (car seats, prams), bun in the oven (dishes, bibs) and bundle of joy (jammies and blankets) gifts.

the dinner for two

THE MOOD	a low-key but enchanting date night at home
THE SCENE	rather than dressing up a corner of the dining table, move a petite table and two chairs to a patio, terrace or rooftop; in cooler months, sit on the floor or sofa fireside in the living room. candle and bud vase: yes. special linens: no.
THE INVITATION	a well-placed phone call and a confident rundown of vitals: saturday. eight o'clock. my place.
THE DRINK	something robust and a little masculine: a manhattan, old-fashioned, sidecar or wine.
THE FOOD	▶ lamb cutlets or chicken marbella (leave out garlic; add potatoes) ▶ roasted tomato and bread soup ▶ chocolate cake
THE PLAYLIST	"trouble in mind" nina simone "l'hotel particulier" serge gainsbourg "rebel rebel" seu jorge "with plenty of money and you" tony bennett
THE EXTRA SOMETHING	play an old-school, two-person board game after your meal. alongside a nightcap, the playful competition is an aphrodisiac. (trust us.)

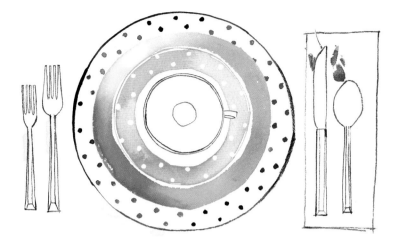

the sunday supper

THE MOOD	a relaxed reentry into the workweek, early enough for a "school night." invite people for five o'clock.
THE INVITATION	a quick ring around to friends on the friday prior
THE DRINKS	▸ champagne cocktail upon arrival ▸ a couple of craft beer options (light and dark) ▸ two mellow wines: one red, one white
THE FOOD	▸ a carving board overflowing with marcona almonds, cheeses and cured meats ▸ grilled fish (summer) ▸ braised short ribs or roast (winter) ▸ a wondrous one-pot dish: chicken tagine, shrimp jambalaya, beef stew (year round) ▸ mediterranean salad
THE PLAYLIST	bebel gilberto's album *tanto tempo* spliced with john coltrane's *ballads*
THE EXTRA SOMETHING	make it a potluck and have your guests bring their favorite dessert.

the garden party

THE MOOD	light and refreshing. play up the simple pleasures of your surroundings.
THE INVITATION	print reproductions of a vintage botanical drawing, changing out the technical information with the event details.
THE SIGNATURE DRINKS	▸ lillet blanc spritzers (lillet blanc + tonic + a squeeze of orange over ice) ▸ champagne on the rocks in tumblers[23] ▸ watermelon lemonade
THE MOBILE FOOD	takeout boxes filled with a selection of picnic food, each personalized with the names of your guests.
THE PLAYLIST	*clambake* (original soundtrack)
THE EXTRA SOMETHING	**SCREEN A FILM** using your smartphone, a rental projector and a cord to connect them. pick something visually or conversationally epic—*three days of the condor, designing woman, the graduate*—and show it against a white wall or white sheet. add a posh popcorn bar with chocolate sea salt, chili-lime and rosemary parmesan toppings. **CELEBRATE CINCO DE MAYO:** ▸ tissue paper flag garlands and paper lanterns in bright hues, or in red, white and green ▸ a gilded piñata ▸ empty salsa jars filled with marigolds and arrangements of cactus flowers on the table ▸ a nacho bar ▸ potluck guacamole ▸ avocado margaritas (blend 1 avocado, 2 cups crushed ice, 1 cup tequila, ½ cup triple sec and 2 peeled limes 'til smooth.)

[23] a drink beloved by marilyn monroe and bill murray.

cocktails in the city

THE MOOD | glittering sophistication

THE INVITATION | paper or e-vitation. make mention of cocktails, confetti and canapés—all shorthand for a swanky evening—and call for sequins and bow ties as the attire.

THE DÉCOR | take visual inspiration from a first-edition book jacket of t. s. eliot's play *the cocktail party* and its two-tone design—a simple serif and sans serif font combination in black and white alongside a bold stroke of gold (or red, depending on the print run).

THE TABLE | small bites on gigantic platters, bowls and pedestals among black tapered candles, low bunches of big white blossoms (like french tulips) in small crystal bowls, thick cocktail napkins.

THE PUNCH | mother's ruin[24]

THE SIGNATURE COCKTAIL | the old cuban *(gleaned from our favorite bartender at bemelmans bar at the carlyle hotel)*

2 oz bacardi 8
5 or 6 fresh mint leaves, plus a sprig for garnish
½ oz fresh lime juice
½ oz simple syrup
2 dashes angostura bitters
ice
1 oz champagne

mix the rum, mint leaves, lime juice, simple syrup and bitters in a shaker. muddle the leaves, then shake the mixture and pour it into a chilled collins glass. add ice. top with champagne. garnish with a sprig of mint.

[24] a drink named after british slang for gin. combine ½ cup granulated sugar, ¾ cup chilled club soda, 1½ cups gin, 1½ cups fresh grapefruit juice, ¾ cup fresh lemon juice, ¾ cup sweet vermouth and 2¼ cup chilled champagne in a large bowl. chill. serve over ice.

THE MOCKTAIL	the moscow mule[25] (minus the vodka)

½ oz fresh lime juice
4 to 6 oz ginger beer
ice
lime slices

THE FIRST ARRIVALS PLAYLIST	"brazil" django reinhardt "foggy notion" the velvet underground "girl from ipanema" stan getz "green onions" booker t. & the m.g.'s "loveless love" louis armstrong

THE LATE NIGHT PLAYLIST	"superstition" stevie wonder "shake it off" taylor swift "the last of the secret agents" nancy sinatra "tainted love" soft cell "oblivion" grimes "this must be the place" talking heads

THE EXTRA SOMETHING	▸ matchbooks custom-printed with a festive word ▸ a photo-ready backdrop to take pictures of everyone upon arrival, when their lipstick and pocket squares are still in place

THE HOLIDAY SEASON TOP-UPS	▸ hang ornaments from a light fixture to transform it into a christmas chandelier. ▸ serve a pot of mulled wine with gingerbread. ▸ crush candy canes in a blender and use the speckled, minty powder on the rims of martinis. ▸ skewer cranberries on drink stirrers and freeze them.

AND PLAYLIST ADDITIONS	"last christmas" wham! "dear santa" mr little jeans

[25] the moscow mule wasn't invented in moscow, but rather at the hotel chatham in manhattan, in 1941.

a tipple & a nibble

the main ingredient in the cocktail
goes with the key ingredient in the dish.

elderflower gimlet ✛ mini cheesecakes

negroni ✛ salted chips, cured meats & cheese

champagne ✛ salmon blinis

manhattan ✛ s'mores

black velvet ✛ mini grilled cheese sandwiches

rob roy ✛ pigs in a blanket (aka: piggy wellingtons)

old-fashioned ✛ pimento cheese sandwiches

pimm's cup ✛ lamb skewers

pisco sour ✛ ceviche

cucumber mojito ✛ spicy tuna rolls

martini ✛ swedish meatballs

gin & tonic ✛ crab cakes

grapefruit pressé ✛ scrambled eggs

sangria ✛ spring rolls

singapore sling ✛ spicy nuts

bloody mary ✛ raw oysters on the half shell

margarita ✛ pot stickers

mother's ruin punch ✛ petit fours

sidecar ✛ devils on horseback

minty gimlet ✛ tomato bruschetta

white wine shandy ✛ samosas

sake ✛ guacamole & chips

dark & stormy ✛ deviled eggs

st-germain & champagne ✛ sliders

moscow mule ✛ fried olives

mint julep ✛ cocktail sausages & mustard

_____ ✛ _____

_____ ✛ _____

_____ ✛ _____

(what's yours?)

"be pretty
   if you can.
be witty
   if you must.
      but
be
gracious
            if it kills you."

ELSIE DE WOLFE

why don't you host...

a midnight birthday supper

what was an after-party in 1898—the year new york city socialite caroline astor invited four hundred people back to her house for an après-theater meal—now has the makings of a (more intimately) indulgent way to celebrate the beginning of a personal new year. on the eve of the special day, after the guest of honor plus three friends (eleven, max) has enjoyed a play or concert, return to the house for an eleven o'clock feast and toast at the stroke of midnight. ties unfastened, heels off and food and drink equal parts glamorous and raffish: a gigantic platter of filet, baguettes and horseradish cream sauce for make-your-own sandwiches; a big bowl of fingerling potatoes with dipping sauce (sour cream, chives, crème fraîche, pancetta); a tower of oysters; bowls of salted nuts; bottles of champagne chilled in an oversize, hotel silver punch bowl filled with ice; ziggurats of tarts and mini cakes for dessert. cheers.

a moveable feast

pick a theme or cuisine, arrange a host for each course—cocktails, entrées, dessert—and party hop between friends' homes over the course of one evening, spending an hour or two at each location. alternatively, take the idea one (no-cook version) further and curate a journey between flavor-compatible bars and restaurants all within a walkable area of a beloved—or intriguing— neighborhood.

a book swap brunch

invite friends to clear out their shelves and coffee tables and exchange their gently used art tomes, memoirs and mysteries over a leisurely buffet and lively raffle. (every book brought equals one ticket. place all the books on a table, and all the corresponding tickets in a bowl— draw to decide the picking order.) at least one person (ideally you) should have a dense, eclectic selection to dispose of.

supply sticky notes and pens for swappers to opine about what they loved about each book and adhere to the covers. separate books by genre with witty signage on library cards and display them flat or vertically so the titles are easily visible on a large table. the finishing touch party favor: canvas tote bags or bookmarks made from strips of heavy satin or grosgrain ribbon. donate leftover books to a neighborhood library or a literary organization.

a new year's day buffet

a low-key, come-and-go afternoon of cozy restorative comfort fare—vegetable soup, rustic bread—and conversation. have new, wooly house socks at the door for guests to switch into upon arrival, and plates of fortune cookies for a twist on dessert.

a pick a day, any day party

when you have an itch to celebrate but no obvious reason to, more than 365 ideas are just a google away. let a search for inspiring figures or out-of-the-box national celebratory days provide your (educationally festive) theme and date. one warm august fourth we celebrated louis armstrong's birthday[26] with an all-new orleans jazz soundtrack, invitations signed "red beans and ricely yours"—just as he signed his letters—and a menu of sazeracs, barbecue and cheese-cake (dishes both lauded in armstrong tunes).

by the same token we've also thrown a midafternoon national donut day[27] fête—and by that we mean a celebratory reason to go buy our first cronuts.

[26] the american jazz trumpeter was born on august 4, 1901.
[27] celebrated since 1938, national donut day is the first friday in june.

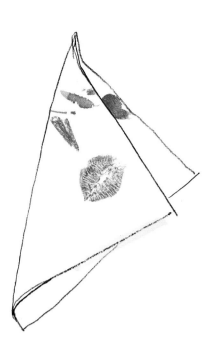

a mystery guest dinner

you invite half the number of guests for the evening.
your guests invite the other half by each bringing
a winsome plus-one that the rest of the guests won't
likely know. order first edition copies of *the mystery
guest*[28] (the ones with pink and red art deco covers)
online for less than one dollar each to set on each plate
as a party favor.

a morning wedding

if you watched prince william and kate middleton's
wedding locally, then you tuned in at eleven in the
morning. in fact, up until the 1880s, it was customary
for all ceremonies to take place around noon. after the
"i do's," guests would gather in someone's home for
brunch, seeing the happy couple off for their honey-
moon at two o'clock.

it's affordable, the morning light is undeniably pretty
and the opportunity for an unconventional reception
is refreshing. given the time of day it could be a picnic,
a gatsby-ish lawn party or a sleek city hall affair (à la
carrie bradshaw and mr. big) followed by brunch at your
favorite local market with bags of small batch coffee
beans and jars of artisanal jam as favors.

plus, it gives the bride a bit of freedom to walk
down the aisle in a shorter, flirtier dress if she likes.
(look up catherine deneuve's, keira knightley's and
audrey hepburn's for inspiration.)

[28] a witty 2006 memoir by french author grégoire bouillier, wherein the narrator
(possibly grégoire) is invited to a birthday party for someone he doesn't know by an
old girlfriend. the party is for an artist (definitely sophie calle), who invites as many
guests as years of life she's celebrating, including a single "mystery guest" who rep-
resents the unknown year ahead. the main character is, unknowingly, that guest.

it's not the night before the party that **a good night's sleep** matters. it's 2 nights before.

WHO'S COMING TO DINNER?

MUSIC TO MY EARS

FAVORITE PARTY OUTFIT:

A PARTY NO-NO:

BEST DANCE SONG:

MY PRE-PARTY RITUAL:

FAVORITE FESTIVE DRINK:

PREFERRED POST-PARTY TRANSPORTATION:

she
cocktail
hand
confett

had a
in her
and
in her
hair.

wining

& dining

let's dish.

add the sauce

& other rules of the kitchen

"everything
in moderation
...including
moderation."
JULIA CHILD

"the only thing
that will make
a soufflé fall is
if it knows you're
afraid of it."
JAMES BEARD

"don't be scared
to fail. if you
haven't set fire to
anything, people
won't know if you
did or not."
SARAH SIMMONS

"always serve too
much hot fudge
sauce on hot fudge
sundaes. it makes
people overjoyed
and puts them in
your debt."
JUDITH OLNEY

"food is an
important part
of a balanced
diet."
FRAN LEBOWITZ

"only the pure
of heart can make
good soup."
BEETHOVEN

have fun.

a little bit of this,
a little bit of that.

cooking is, we think, a sensory science. you could meticulously measure the margarine, time your tagliatelle to the nanosecond and pulse your plum tomatoes to a plump pulp, but following the recipe to a T is no guarantee that your marinara will actually taste any good.[1]

we find inspiration in the way our moms, grandmothers and great-grandmothers cooked—maybe dads and grandfathers, too. some tossed meals together entirely without recipes or with ones passed on verbally and changed along the way.

sometimes we grab a recipe and then don't follow it, taking out what we don't like and throwing in what we do. we're not the only ones. sarah simmons, who opened the culinary salon, city grit, in 2010 because she wanted the flexibility of cooking different food every day, is a strong advocate for playing with your food. "take marcella hazan's famous tomato sauce—nothing but tomatoes, butter and onion," she suggests, "and throw in garam masala, curry, coconut milk, thai chiles and oregano." today you'll find her at her newest venture, birds & bubbles, pairing fried chicken and champagne.

to re-create a dish you had elsewhere, begin with the key ingredient. then "find recipes on the internet that

toss-it-together
chicken soup

- skinless chicken breast
  - garlic
  - broccoli
  - onion
  - rice
  - carrots
  - salt
  - pepper
- water or broth

a friend of
a friend's aunt's
salmon dip

- cream cheese, at room temperature
- a handful of chopped green onions
- a big spoonful of ketchup
  - a smaller spoonful of horseradish
- 1 8oz can of salmon, drained and flaked

blend cream cheese, onions, horseradish and ketchup till well mixed. fold in salmon and mix well.

[1] the human tongue has between two thousand and eight thousand tastebuds. each lasts, on average, ten days. not only are your tastebuds always changing, but so is the potency of the ingredients you're cooking with depending on what's in season. high altitudes, meanwhile, can also affect the quality of your baked goods.

prepare and bake
a box of devil's food
cake mix according to the
package directions.

once cool, transfer one
layer to a cake plate
and poke a few holes
in it with the handle of
a wooden spoon.

pour a full jar of caramel
sauce over it, completely
filling the holes.

sprinkle a smashed
toffee bar over the top.

set the second cake layer
over the caramel and toffee
and frost both layers with
dark fudge frosting.

are in that family and look for consistencies in the ingredients and the techniques," says simmons. mind you, some are easier to replicate than others: after digging into one stunningly delicious apple crumble at a small beachside diner in miami—and then day-dreaming about it far too long after the vacation was over—it took a handful of tries (and a friend later bringing one to new york in her carry-on) before we stumbled upon the golden ingredient. turns out, it was a handful of cranberries. the hilarity of the process made the eureka bite absolutely worth it.

similarly, to drum up something delicious on the fly, start with a base (chicken, rice, beef, kale, chocolate, etc.) and start adding ingredients to it. put in a little of this, a little of that and ask yourself, "does it taste good?" a few times as you do. you might even feel inspired to throw in things that don't seem like they should go together. if there's one thing that a new york chopped salad station has taught us, it's that raisins, smoked bacon, edamame and avocado make a good team.

when it comes to food, making something from nothing[2] is a very good skill to have.

[2] in 1937, the owner of the brown derby restaurant in hollywood found himself in need of a snack after closing time. and so he rummaged through the kitchen, pulled out this and that, started chopping and threw it all in a bowl. thus was born the cobb salad.

HOW TO: *whip fresh cream*

the finishing touch for pies, puddings, hot cocoa and irish coffees.

1. place a metal bowl and a whisk or hand mixer attachments in the freezer.

2. when you're ready for dessert, pour 1 pint heavy cream into the chilled bowl and whisk vigorously until it becomes cloudy and smooth.

3. as it thickens, add 2 tablespoons confectioners' sugar.

4. (optional but delightful) whirl in vanilla extract, citrus zest or a sprinkle of cinnamon.

5. spoon dollops directly atop your plated dessert or, more fun, bring the whole bowl to the table and let guests spatula a billow or two out themselves.

HOW TO: *make a vinaigrette*

1. mix a concoction of roughly four parts olive oil to one part vinegar. (experiment with red, white, cider, rice or, our favorite, champagne vinegar.)

2. add a few squeezes of lemon, a couple grinds of pepper and a pinch of salt.

3. mix everything together with a fork right in the empty salad bowl.

4. top with salad greens and toss.

12 ingredients that go with everything

- salt
- onions
- bacon
- garlic
- wine
- cream
- olive oil
- shallots
- fresh olives
- salty nuts
- cornichons
- cheese

WHAT DO YOU GET WHEN YOU COMBINE THE ESSENCES OF BANANA, RASPBERRY, LEMON AND PINEAPPLE? STRAWBERRY.

HOW TO: *flambé*

setting your food on fire is a fun party trick for the dessert course (think baked alaska, baba au rhum, bananas foster) but the technique also boosts the flavors of chicken (with sweet vermouth), shrimp (with cognac) and filet mignon (with brandy), a midcentury favorite called steak diane.

1. roll up your sleeves and tie back your hair. (you are dealing with liquid that is on fire.)

2. turn off your stove's overhead fan (all fans, really) and all but the one burner you're using.

3. place whatever you're flambéing in a large, shallow, preheated skillet and set on a flat surface away from the stove.

4. pour a room-temperature, 80-proof spirit over the dessert, let it soak for a few seconds, no more.

5. using a long barbecue lighter or fireplace match, ignite the fumes at the edge of the skillet.

6. lightly shake or spoon-stir the now-flaming skillet to distribute the alcohol and the heat throughout your fruit[3] or protein.

7. let cook for 15 to 30 seconds, until the flame goes out on its own.

8. serve the flambéed ingredient immediately.

the flavor palette

there are a range of flavor tastes (salty, sweet, sour, bitter, savory), smells and physical traits ("heat" and "cold") that you experience at different points while you eat.

flavorists call the tastes and traits "notes," much like a perfume, the "top note" being the first thing you taste, the "bottom note" being the last. so mix and match from the palette to create (seemingly) endless flavor combinations.

---

[3] fruit flambé of any kind (banana, fig, mango) is mighty fine atop ice cream, yogurt, cheese, pancakes, even a savory protein.

what's in your pantry

"A GOOD COOK IS LIKE A SORCERESS WHO DISPENSES HAPPINESS." *elsa schiaparelli*

ALISON CAYNE
owner, haven's kitchen
new york city

sea salt

unbleached flour

whole
black peppercorns

whole
grain mustard

Shoyo

toasted ses. oil

sesame seeds

tahini

crushed tomatoes

Vegan bouillon cubes

Whole caraway,
coriander

Hotsauce

Fishsauce

Honey

Maple syrup

Beans! Nuts!

KARI MORRIS
founder, morris kitchen
new york city

PRESERVED LEMON

ALMOND BUTTER
PIONEER SQUARE
PANTRY

KEWPIE MAYO

APPLE CIDER
VINEGAR
SPARROW LANE

TIN'S SMOOTH
MUSTARD

MALDON
SEA SALT

NOCI BELLA
WALNUT BARS

POMI TOMATOES

SFOGLINI PASTA

FRANKIE'S
OLIVE OIL

SARAH SIMMONS
owner and head chef
birds & bubbles
new york city

Olive oil
from georgia olive farms

jacobsen Salt Co.
finishing salt

la boîte spices
(dali, cataluna and ana
are my favorites!)

dried limes

beluga lentils

carolina gold rice

heirloom benne seeds

white balsamic vinegar

milkwood hot sauce

red boat anchovy salt

twenty-one things to do with tomatoes

▶ slice and sprinkle with sugar.

▶ bake a tomato pie: layer slices of tomato and three cheeses between two pie crusts. top with olive oil and salt.

▶ chop alongside bell peppers and onion and mash with ground meat for a tasty burger patty.

▶ hollow a beefsteak tomato and stuff with sausage, garlic and cooked rice. top with cheese and then bake.

▶ chop and toss with balsamic vinegar, lemon juice, olive oil, salt, pepper and fresh basil.

▶ roast with garlic and bacon in the oven. blend in a mixer to make soup. top with parmesan.

▶ slice heirloom tomatoes extra thin and sprinkle with sea salt for tomato carpaccio.

▶ top breakfast toast with charred tomato slices and a fried egg.

▶ mix cherry tomatoes with roasted corn and avocado for a salad.

▶ make a caprese salad by alternating slices with fresh basil and mozzarella.

▶ oven dry and refrigerate to use in salads and on sandwiches, antipasti plates

▶ make gazpacho on a hot summer day.

▶ BLTs. (we like ours with slices of avocado.)

▶ slice and use as the finishing touch atop a piece of toasted crusty bread thinly covered in mayonnaise.

▶ chop and cook down until they're super sweet and nearly jammy. (put this on everything.)

▶ stuff cherry tomatoes with goat cheese.

▶ skewer on sticks alongside peppers, onion and pineapple, and grill or broil.

▶ pulse in a food processor with garlic, onion, 1 jalapeno pepper, 1 anaheim pepper and lemon to make salsa.

▶ chop, salt and place in a strainer over a bowl to drain. use the tomatoes for sauce and refrigerate the liquid to use in cocktails— like bloody marys.

▶ chop and stir fry in a wok with oil, eggs and green onion.

▶ bake plum tomatoes with onion, bell pepper, garlic, cumin, paprika, feta cheese and eggs in a skillet.

"the discovery of **a new** dish does more for the **happiness** of the human race than the discovery of a star."

JEAN-ANTHELME BRILLAT-SAVARIN

it takes a meal to create a village

"I DON'T KNOW WHY, BUT IF YOU GO TO SOMEBODY'S HOUSE AND THEY'RE MAKING SOMETHING, THEY USUALLY SAY INTERESTING THINGS WHILE THEY'RE COOKING." *christopher walken*

at my restaurant, **THE SMILE,** there's a window from the kitchen into the dining room, so i can see the energy in the room while i cook. that's really the payoff for a chef. the tables aren't too close together or too far apart, so people can have a private conversation. the lighting is low, but not dark. it feels like a cozy embrace.

i hope it's the kind of menu where you have a favorite item that you come back for—the granola at breakfast, the meatballs at dinner. nothing's too rich, too restaurant-y or has too many layers of sauce, so you don't get sick of the selection and the dishes don't feel like they're coming out of a giant kitchen filled with a lot of chefs. because they aren't.

likewise at home, my kitchen is in a mezzanine overlooking the dining room, so people can come up and talk to me while i cook, or i can talk over the balcony. so when friends or family are over, the food—preparing it and serving it—becomes the activity. i always serve family-style. it seems more natural and that's the way my style of food is best served, too. i'm not creating perfect portions. plus, it's nice to pass the dishes, interact, serve other people. it creates dialogue."

MELIA MARDEN *is the co-owner and executive chef of the smile, a townhouse-turned-restaurant in downtown manhattan. a stone's throw away, her east village apartment features a twelve-person broccoli green dining table and an open kitchen with maraschino red tiles and cotton-candy pink cabinets. together, they act as a laboratory for her unfussy, delicious recipes.*

melia's toolkit

- vintage ceramic restaurant tip trays, collected on eBay and repurposed as small prep bowls for chopped herbs and onions

- a microplane grater for zesting citrus peel and finely grating cheese

- classic french enamelware canisters for storing sugar, peppercorns and salt

- kitchen tongs for sautéing

- restaurant sheet pans for roasting meat, chicken and vegetables

- a 5-quart cast-iron le creuset braiser— an all-purpose item to cook just about everything in

anatomy of a cheese plate

"buy on apples, sell on cheese" is an old wine industry saying. apples emphasize faults in wine; cheese, meanwhile, enhances its finer qualities. but not all cheese is created equal. hard cheeses (cheddar, gruyere) are easy to pair with wines. soft cheeses (brie) are trickier, but should still make an appearance for their deliciousness. apples should not.

say

the basics

plan on 2oz of cheese per person.

3 is your magic number, each one made with either a different type of milk—sheep, cow, goat's milk—or all the same:

▶ 1 soft and creamy cheese (such as a brie or camembert)
▶ 1 firm cheese (such as cheddar or gouda)
▶ 1 hard cheese (like parmigiano-reggiano)

don't crowd the plate: serve your selection on one or two large shared platters—or an individual tidbit plate per guest.

have one knife per cheese.

include plain bread (baguette, sourdough) or neutral crackers in a separate basket, or pick a bread with walnuts, dried fruit or olives, which pair well with cheese.

CHEESE IS BEST SERVED AT ROOM TEMPERATURE, SO PULL IT OUT OF THE REFRIGERATOR AN HOUR BEFORE SERVING TIME.

the aperitif cheese plate

before dinner, mix lighter cheeses (herb-coated goat cheese, buffalo mozzarella) with savory sides:

▶ olives
▶ prosciutto
▶ cornichons
▶ walnuts
▶ tomato and caramelized onion jam, or fig chutney

the dessert cheese plate

end on a full-flavored note, with rich cheeses (manchego, cheddar, gouda, blue) and sweet treats:

▶ marcona almonds (toss with a bit of oil and salt if they aren't already)
▶ fig or raspberry jam
▶ honey or real maple syrup
▶ dried or slices of fresh fruit (pears, figs or raspberries)

the alternatives

slice the top off a whole brie or camembert, then layer with dried dates, apricots or peaches.

serve a big basket of salty, savory gougères (pronounced GOO-zhair)— a bite-sized combination of salty gruyere cheese and flakey puff pastry— swaddled in linen to keep them warm.

on wining and dining

we sometimes buy books for their beautiful covers and, occasionally, wines for their labels. they make for great conversation pieces. (the velvet devil's label, reminiscent of a beatnik-era concert poster, is a current favorite.)

buy by the box.
while twelve delicious bottles in a cardboard box doesn't sound like spontaneous living, it does have its benefits:

▶ at every gathering, you will serve more than you planned.
▶ a box encourages you to try new varieties.
▶ you will always have a gift to bring to impromptu parties.
▶ you never know what you might cook, so diversity is practicality.
▶ for every degree the temperature drops in winter, the wine shop moves a block farther away. in new york city, it moves two.

HOW TO: *cook with wine*

when a recipe calls for red wine, use a young, full wine such as a zinfandel or a chianti. for white, grab one that's dry and full bodied, such as a sauvignon blanc. or, use a dry white french vermouth instead.

cheese fondue

ingredients

8 oz emmenthal cheese
8 oz gruyere cheese
8 oz appenzeller or
    raclette cheese
2 tbsp cornstarch or flour
1 garlic clove
1 cup dry white wine
1 tbsp lemon juice
pinch of freshly ground
    black pepper
pinch of freshly grated
    nutmeg

grate all the cheese into a medium bowl and toss in the cornstarch.

cut the garlic clove in half and rub the cut sides over the bottom of a saucepan. discard the garlic.

pour the wine and lemon juice into a saucepan and bring to a gentle simmer on the stove.

add large handfuls of the grated cheese, one at a time, and stir until melted.

repeat until the cheese has melted and the fondue is smooth.

add the pepper and nutmeg. stir.

pour the mixture into the fondue pot.

light the fondue burner and place the pot on top over low heat (just enough to keep the cheese warm and liquid).

enjoy!

HOW TO: *eat fondue*

1. spear, dip, twirl, drip, eat.

2. avoid touching your lips to the fork or double-dipping. (it is a communal pot.)

3. keep your eye on the prize: fondue tradition states that if a woman loses a piece of food in the pot, she has to kiss every man at the table. if a man does, he must gift the hostess a bottle of very good wine.

Green Grocer Stoke Newington?
↱ Borough Market — Alice to
      Call

Dinner 23.10.14

Fig & Stichelton
Beetroot & Goats Curd   one more for (n)
                               dairy / vegan!

Plants!
Call Nic @
Grace & Thorn

options — Ceviche?
         Jerusalem Artichoke?

✳ Lamb & Cauliflower ✓   Salsa? / with Nuts?
                               Pesto?

Ⓥ — Squash + Pistachio Pesto   different to the Next
                               Main!

Lemon Posset & Berry Compote / ginger
                               shortbread

No. Dairy — Coconut yoghurt / berry + shortbread !
         ↳ Call grocery to see if they have Co-yo!

— Napkins
— Flowers — forage / twigs   → Hackney Marshes
— Type Menus
— Type Thank you's   ↳ Kingsland Rd for paper   Need Car!

— WINE / BOOZE!   — Call Andy / wine Merchants
— Bistro glasses   Andy glasses too?   collect Thurs / Friday?
— Table / Bench Collection — CALL Lisa

— Kim do you have Water glasses / table cloths?
Alice — Bring Table cloths
Laura — Collect Plants.

how we met

"we each had rival stalls at a charity jumble sale. our mutual friend, chef gizzi erskine, was making a big pot of chili so we stood and ate and started chatting. we soon discovered our mutual love of food and cooking. then we bonded over a pair of dungarees and a cat-print blouse at the sale. that sort of bond can't be broken."

for the love of (self-taught) cooking

ALICE:
"i'm very much a cook, not a chef. my mum is also self-taught but had a company that made gorgeous vegetarian food for small events. growing up our house centered around cooking. she gave me the confidence to give this a go."

LAURA:
"i've been baking at home since i could walk, leaving a trail of flour mixture in my wake—much to my mum's dismay when it came time to clean up. since then, she's passed her old recipes to me and my sisters, and now i pass my new recipes on to her. my dad is also a keen foodie and my boyfriend is a vegetarian, so my eyes are always open to new ways of cooking."

every supper club we throw has a different look and feel inspired by the time of year, what's in season, what we've seen and what we've eaten that month. we are forever tearing out pages, bookmarking, scribbling notes and sending each other screen grabs, photos and instagrams of color combinations, flavor pairings, menus we've spied and ingredients we've seen in a market stall. a color palette in a piece of art at the tate modern might even inspire us to re-create it in a salad.

we always choose things for the menu that we've never made before. the plethora of amazing restaurants on our doorstep—indian, israeli, turkish, modern british, japanese, venetian, french—are constant inspiration. we'll interpret elements into new dishes of our own, and also modify dishes that were served at our own family tables and practice them until we get them just right. twelve lemon tarts or three hare ragus later, it feels so satisfying to have mastered a new skill.

recently, we brought back twenty mini milk bottles in a suitcase from australia to serve gazpacho in and incredible hand-woven napkins from mexico city. closer to home, we scoured charity shops and found antique platters for less than twenty dollars. these little touches make all the difference, and we treasure the process of finding them! we want people to feel like they've tried something new—whether it be turning up to a random flat for dinner with nineteen other people or the food itself. our events are open to anyone, so we get an incredible mix of people. that we want them to feel like they're going to a friend's house rather than booking a table in a restaurant is probably why we are still shooing people out at two a.m. sometimes!"

ALICE LEVINE AND LAURA JACKSON *are best friends, foodies, a radio host and television presenter—respectively— and co-founders of the jackson & levine supper club. every two months in east london they host feasts that are almost way too pretty to eat. (almost.)*

HOW TO: *pan-sear steak*

"fast and high" is your mantra for cooking a cut of beef at home: caramelized and crusty on the outside and moist, medium-rare-ish on the inside.

1. take a 2-inch-thick,[4] well-marbled rib eye, filet mignon, t-bone or new york strip out of the refrigerator roughly an hour before you want to serve it and immediately season it liberally with kosher salt and freshly cracked black pepper.

2. place a 10-inch stainless-steel or cast-iron pan on your burner.

3. turn up the heat to high and add 1 tablespoon of oil.

4. once the oil is shimmery and rippling, put the steak in and cook for about 1 minute, then reduce the heat to medium-high and cook for a minute more.

5. flip your steak with tongs, turn the temperature up to high and cook for a minute more.

6. transfer the steak to a platter and let rest for 5 to 10 minutes.

7. serve!

[4] this might seem like a lot of beef, but it's actually better to cook one large steak for two people than to cook two smaller steaks.

HOW TO: *Make a pan sauce*

after you've browned meat, poultry or fish, make a matching gravy in the same pan.

the virtues of
mise en place

translating literally to "putting in place," this french phrase has a special, even philosophical, meaning for chefs.

before turning on a single burner, they will have every ingredient and tool at the ready— buttered and butterflied, julienned and juiced, cleaned and carved— within arm's reach.

try it—we find it does make the process rather symphonic. say it with us: "mees-on-plass."

1. in your stainless-steel skillet, retain a tablespoon or two of the fat leftover from browning the meat. add a little extra olive oil or butter if need be.

2. add diced shallots or onions and sauté for a minute.

3. add a shot or two of red or white wine and bring the mixture to a simmer over medium heat.

4. using a wooden spoon, scrape the leftover brown bits from the bottom of the pan (what chefs call the "fond") and incorporate them into the sauce.

5. let the sauce simmer and cook down for a few minutes.

6. pour in 1 cup chicken stock and let that reduce for a few minutes more.

7. remove the pan from the heat and whisk in cubes of cold butter. add fresh herbs, if you have them.

8. season with salt and pepper and pour the sauce over the meat.

a dish for a dish

"cooking is like love. it should be entered into with abandon or not at all," began **HARRIET VAN HORNE** in an article the newspaper columnist wrote for *vogue* in 1956, wherein she offered "six recipes, simple, honest, and sometimes unconventional."

it's funny how, almost in return, simple, unusual recipes provoke our fondest memories. they could be part of a larger cultural consciousness—a shared recollection of the yam casserole our friends' moms served some variation of at thanksgivings growing up (baked yams, cranberries, brown sugar, cinnamon and oats, sometimes topped with browned marshmallows)—or in a personal experience we quietly hold dear.

our food histories connect us emotionally. we like the idea of starting our own traditions, too.

emily spivack's
vegetarian borscht

i've spent new year's eve with the same group of friends for the past eight years. we usually rent a house in the berkshires and do lots of cooking, hanging out by the fire and playing word games.

one year, i got a later start driving up there from brooklyn. it was pitch black. i didn't have cell reception and there was a bad snowstorm. it was treacherous.

i finally arrived around midnight, hungry, tired and hours later than i'd planned. i found my friends drinking wine and talking around the dinner table. my friend amanda said, 'i have borscht waiting for you.' she'd made two versions of the soup: one with meat and one for vegetarians like me.

for no particular reason, i'd never had borscht before. i tried to hide my confusion and thought, 'cold soup in a blizzard?'

and yet it was the best thing to eat at that moment: hearty, invigorating and warm. red and gold beets, carrots, potatoes.

the entire long weekend i kept coming back to the borscht. it was the perfect thing after sledding and snowshoeing. and so, ever since then, i ask amanda to make it for new year's.

this year we changed up the tradition and gathered in palm springs. and the menu changed, too. that's when i realized just how much i loved—and expected — the borscht."

EMILY SPIVACK *is an artist and writer. she's the author of* worn stories *and editor of* threaded, *the smithsonian's clothing history blog.*

INGREDIENTS

2 lbs beets
olive oil
½ head garlic, minced
2 onions, chopped
salt
freshly ground black pepper
1 tbsp caraway seeds
2 russet or yukon gold
    potatoes, peeled and cut
    into cubes
2 to 3 parsnips, sliced
head green cabbage,
    chopped (optional)
2 to 3 carrots, sliced
dill (fresh, ideally)
4 to 6 cups vegetable stock
    (or more)
red wine vinegar
1 can peeled whole tomatoes,
    chopped
fresh lemon juice

sour cream and black bread
    for serving

DIRECTIONS

the vegetables are very adjustable, so feel free to leave something out if you don't like it.

wash and trim the beets (but don't peel them), wrap in aluminum foil and place them in a pan. roast in the oven at 400°f until tender—poke one with a fork every 30 minutes
to check.

in a heavy pot, sauté the garlic in olive oil. add the onions, salt, pepper and caraway seeds and cook until the onion becomes slightly brown and fragrant. add the potatoes, then add the parsnips, cabbage and carrots in that order, stirring and letting each cook a bit before adding the next one. add dill.

add the stock, a few shakes of red wine vinegar and the tomatoes, including the juice from the can. cook until the potatoes and parsnips are soft. add a dash of salt, pepper, red wine vinegar, lemon juice, and more dill and caraway seeds as desired. cover and stir occasionally.

once the beets are ready, take them out of the oven, unwrap the foil and let them cool enough to handle. peel by squinching the skins off. (your hands will turn magenta.) chop the beets into cubes.

throw the beets into the pot (the soup will turn pink!) and simmer over low heat as long as you like. it's delicious hot or cold. upon serving, garnish with a dollop of sour cream and fresh dill and serve with black bread.

p.s. it will only get more delicious over the next few days in the fridge.

ebony bizys' temaki rolls

"

i used to host temaki parties in my little sydney apartment long before i moved to tokyo. i like to think of temaki as japan's answer to family taco nights. *'te'* translates as 'hand' and *'maki'* is japanese for 'roll.' now that i'm a local, a temaki party at hello sandwich HQ is often put together in a moment's notice. i love putting little plates to use, mixing and matching polka dot and striped ceramics to lay out the ingredients. guests can pick and choose what they like, so i never have to worry if so-and-so can eat fish or so on. it's always colorful and playful, and there's always one or two people who will put too much on their roll and have trouble holding it all together, which inspires more than one round of laughter."

EBONY BIZYS *is an australian craft artist, designer and voice of the blog* hello sandwich *in tokyo.*

INGREDIENTS
temaki nori (or get regular
  nori sheets and cut in half)
steamed japanese rice
japanese mayonnaise
cucumbers, peeled and
  cut into sticks
lettuce
carrots, cut into sticks
spring onion, sliced
avocado, sliced
shiso leaves
sprouts

optional: other ingredients
for the fillings such as tuna,
prawns, sashimi, tamagoyaki
(japanese omelette) and
karage (fried chicken).

DIRECTIONS
serve all of the ingredients at left on pretty ceramics. guests create their own temaki by placing fillings of their choice onto one end of a nori sheet and rolling into a cone. (if they want their nori to stay crispy, add lettuce to the nori first and then their rice.)

amirah kassem's

fluffy white icing

food was such a huge part of my growing up and my mom has always made my birthday cakes. in fact, i've never thought of baking as a skill because it was so normal to me.

for my sixth birthday, my mom made me a little mermaid cake. she was into every detail: the cake was five feet tall, and her icing hair looked like it was blowing in the wind. she also made my brother his own little cake in the shape of flounder that was in perfect proportion to ariel.

i don't remember anything else about that party except that cake. licking icing off my fingers brings back so many good memories."

AMIRAH KASSEM *is the owner of brooklyn's flour shop.*

INGREDIENTS

½ cup water
1½ tbsp light corn syrup
1½ cups sugar
½ tsp salt
½ tsp cream of tartar
2 egg whites
1½ tsp vanilla

DIRECTIONS

place the first five ingredients into a saucepan or large tea kettle with a pouring lip. stir over medium heat until sugar is completely dissolved.

place the egg whites in a separate bowl and beat on the highest speed until egg whites begin to hold their shape. (if you're using a mixer bowl, use the whip attachment.) continue on the highest speed and pour the hot syrup into bowl in a fine stream. add vanilla and continue beating for another 5 minutes or until frosting loses its sheen and stands in stiff peaks. frost cake immediately.

YIELDS: enough for three 9-inch layers.

YOU CAN ALSO ADD: crushed peppermint candy (1 cup worth) or lemon (mix 6 tbsp water, 2 tbsp lemon juice and ¼ tsp grated lemon rind) just before frosting.

off the charts*

UNIT	EQUALS			
4 cups	2 pints	1 quart	¼ gallon	----
2 cups	1 pint	½ quart	----	----
1 cup	8 fl oz	16 tsbp	48 tsp	237 ml
¾ cup	6 fl oz	12 tsbp	36 tsp	177 ml
⅔ cup	5 fl oz	11 tsbp	32 tsp	158 ml
½ cup	4 fl oz	8 tsbp	24 tsp	118 ml
⅓ cup	3 fl oz	5 tsbp	16 tsp	79 ml
¼ cup	2 fl oz	4 tsbp	12 tsp	59 ml
⅛ cup	1 fl oz	2 tsbp	6 tsp	30 ml
1/16 cup	½ fl oz	1 tsbp	3 tsp	15 ml

*and if all else fails, order takeout.

"DOST THOU THINK, BECAUSE THOU ART VIRTUOUS, THAT THERE SHALL BE NO MORE CAKES AND ALE?" *william shakespeare, twelfth night*

jeralyn gerba's great-aunt's
french chocolate cake

never was a guest more welcome at the dinner table than my great-aunt helen was with her delicious chocolate cake. my great-aunt guarded her recipe for decades. she knew it was her surefire way to be invited to every party. she got it from the recipe section of *the daily news* in the 1950s and amended it, with the directive to only use the finest ingredients and mix everything by hand. she'd serve it in wedges with dollops of fresh cream. its elegance lies in its nonchalance—once baked, a crack emerges down the center of the cake—and it pairs equally well with a glass of sherry in the wee hours of the evening as it does with a cup of tea at breakfast the next day. i'm known to do both."

JERALYN GERBA *is the editorial director and co-founder of the travel website* fathom.

INGREDIENTS
½ cup french cocoa
   dissolved in
   ¾ cup boiling water
½ cup sweet butter
2 cups sugar
1 tsp vanilla
½ tsp baking soda
½ cup dairy sour cream
2 cups sifted cake flour
   (king arthur brand
   or swan's down)
⅛ tsp salt
3 egg whites, stiffly beaten

DIRECTIONS
pre-heat the oven to 350°f.

with the dissolved cocoa at the ready, cream butter and sugar in a separate bowl.

add cocoa mixture and vanilla. add baking soda and sour cream, and blend well. beat in flour and salt. fold in egg whites.

turn into two well-greased and floured 9-inch cake pans and bake until the cake begins to leave the sides of the pan (approximately 25 minutes).

you'll know the cake is truly finished when the dough cracks on top. serve with freshly whipped cream.

cassi bryn-michalik's
anchovy dipping oil

in the 1940s, writers and artists began spending time in the cote d'azur. a tiny restaurant and inn called colombe d'or became one of their places to meet. joan miró, georges braque, marc chagall and pablo picasso, among others, would exchange art for room and board. it still attracts creatives today, and some of my fondest memories are of alfresco lunches there with friends and family.

you dine amongst incredible art—one of alexander calder's mobiles hangs by the swimming pool—and the food is deliciously french. one of the best dishes is the crudité. what i love about this huge bowl full of gorgeous vegetables—a whole artichoke, bell peppers, enormous stalks of celery, cucumber and a bundle of radishes—is that everything isn't cut up into ready-to-eat pieces. you have to do some of the slicing and dicing yourself and the experience of doing that over conversation is so chic and perfectly french. it's become my favorite thing to put on my own table when i'm having a party or friends over for dinner, served with a nice warm anchovy dipping oil."

CASSI BRYN-MICHALIK *is a trend-forecaster and travel, style and culture writer in paris.*

INGREDIENTS
1 cup extra-virgin olive oil
½ cup unsalted butter
8 canned anchovy fillets, chopped
3 garlic cloves, finely chopped

DIRECTIONS
heat ingredients in a heavy medium skillet over low heat until butter melts and mixture begins to simmer, about three minutes. season with salt and pepper. transfer to a flameproof bowl, such as a fondue pot. place bowl over candle or canned heat burner. serve with vegetables you love, leaving some of them whole to show off their beauty.

take
three ingredients

to a few odds and ends from your larder
(olive oil, sea salt, freshly cracked black pepper),
add just three more tasty foodstuffs to create these
nonchalant starters, mains, even desserts.

starters

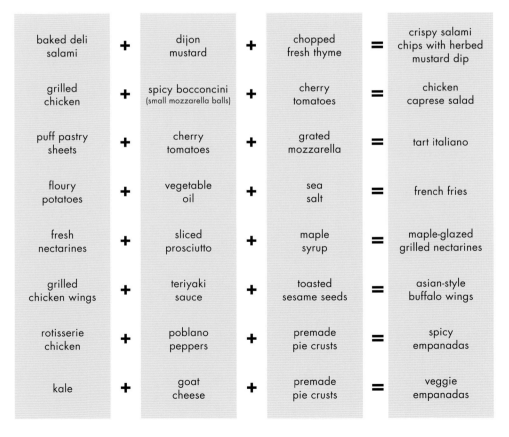

						=	
baked deli salami	+	dijon mustard	+	chopped fresh thyme	=	crispy salami chips with herbed mustard dip
grilled chicken	+	spicy bocconcini (small mozzarella balls)	+	cherry tomatoes	=	chicken caprese salad
puff pastry sheets	+	cherry tomatoes	+	grated mozzarella	=	tart italiano
floury potatoes	+	vegetable oil	+	sea salt	=	french fries
fresh nectarines	+	sliced prosciutto	+	maple syrup	=	maple-glazed grilled nectarines
grilled chicken wings	+	teriyaki sauce	+	toasted sesame seeds	=	asian-style buffalo wings
rotisserie chicken	+	poblano peppers	+	premade pie crusts	=	spicy empanadas
kale	+	goat cheese	+	premade pie crusts	=	veggie empanadas

mains

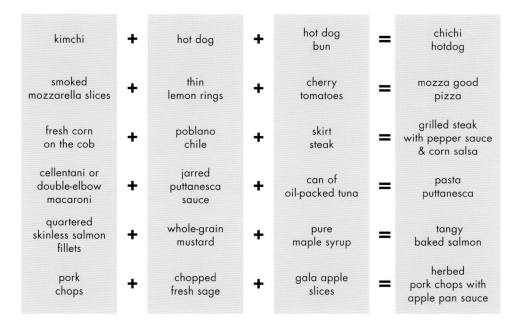

kimchi	+	hot dog	+	hot dog bun	= chichi hotdog

kimchi + hot dog + hot dog bun = chichi hotdog

smoked mozzarella slices + thin lemon rings + cherry tomatoes = mozza good pizza

fresh corn on the cob + poblano chile + skirt steak = grilled steak with pepper sauce & corn salsa

cellentani or double-elbow macaroni + jarred puttanesca sauce + can of oil-packed tuna = pasta puttanesca

quartered skinless salmon fillets + whole-grain mustard + pure maple syrup = tangy baked salmon

pork chops + chopped fresh sage + gala apple slices = herbed pork chops with apple pan sauce

desserts

1 package chocolate wafers + 3 (8-oz) packages cream cheese + 1 cup chocolate syrup = icebox chocolate cheesecake

4 cups fresh blackberries + 2 cups sugar + 1 puff pastry sheet = summer berry tarts

jar of nutella + 4 eggs + nuts = chocolate-hazelnut brownies

bittersweet chocolate + 2 large eggs + heavy cream = chocolate mousse supreme

HOW TO: *Shuck an oyster*

this delicate art was perfected by a brawny breed.

1. wash a bag of freshly harvested oysters under cold running water to remove grit and then place in ice for 1 hour.

2. put on a set of chainmail shucking gloves (they're oddly glamorous) or, in a pinch, cover one hand with a folded kitchen towel.

3. place an oyster in one protected hand with the rounded cup side down in your palm and the narrower hinged point toward you.

4. grab an oyster knife with your other hand. insert it into the hinge, just between the shells, and, with gentle pressure, twist the blade to pop the shell open.

5. run the blade over the meat along the top of the shell to sever the oyster from its top shell. continue using a twisting motion to separate the top and bottom shells.

6. lift off the top shell and discard.

7. cut under the oyster to release it from the bottom of the shell, being careful to keep as much liquid in the shell as possible.

8. place the opened oyster on a bed of crushed ice and repeat steps 3 to 8 until you've shucked at least a dozen.

why don't you...

▸ bake dozens of cheese straws and freeze them in
batches of twenty-five. (pull out and re-heat in the oven
when unexpected guests pop over.)

▸ sprinkle coarse sea salt on top of warm chocolate
chip cookies, klondike bars and croissants.

▸ pile thinly sliced strips of potatoes onto a waffle iron
to make hashbrowns.

▸ freeze whipped cream on a cookie sheet, cut out heart
shapes with a cookie cutter and drop them into mugs of
hot chocolate.

▸ use the bottom of a crystal glass to imprint shortbread
cookies before baking.

▸ make open-faced sandwiches with ingredients in your
favorite colors.

▸ make monogram pancakes by filling a turkey baster
with the batter and "drawing" letters into the skillet.
or, try pancake pops (mini pancakes on popsicle sticks)

▸ make a pumpkin pie without the crust. (pumpkin
custard!)

▸ bake cookies in a muffin tin to make them soft and
uniform. then serve them warm atop shot glasses of
cold milk.

▸ top breakfast toast with lunch fillings like avocado,
shrimp or tuna salad.

▸ toast sushi rice to use on salads in lieu of croutons

▸ pickle it.

"COOKING IS AN ART, BUT ALL ART REQUIRES KNOWING SOMETHING ABOUT THE TECHNIQUES AND MATERIALS."
nathan myhrvold, author of *modernist cuisine*, a 2,438-page book on science-driven cooking.

HOW TO: *poach an egg*

an easy, satisfying toast, pasta and salad topper.

1. fill a saucepan two-thirds full with water.

2. bring the water to a boil, then turn heat down until you get a steady simmering.

3. crack the eggs individually into a measuring cup with a handle. super-fresh eggs only, please.

4. add a small dash of rice vinegar or other mild vinegar to the water.

5. create a gentle whirlpool in the water to help the egg white wrap around the yolk.

6. slowly lower the measuring cup into the water and then tip the egg out, white first. leave to cook for 3 to 4 minutes, depending on how runny or firm you like your eggs.

7. remove the egg with a slotted spoon, pat it dry with a paper towel and gently cut off any wispy edges.

8. season and enjoy at once!

 for an eggs benedict brunch, poach several eggs at once by cracking them into separate cups and slipping them into the water one by one. extend the cooking time by about 30 seconds for each extra egg.

eat cake for break-fast.

"LET'S FACE IT, A NICE CREAMY CHOCOLATE CAKE DOES A LOT FOR A LOT OF PEOPLE; IT DOES FOR ME." *audrey hepburn*

here's how to cut one.[5]

1. rinse a 12- to 14-inch thin-bladed serrated knife in very hot water.

2. measure out the number of slices by scoring them on the cake's surface, using the knife's edge to gently mark where you'll cut.

3a. round cakes: think of the cake like a clock. plunge in the tip of the knife at 12:00 and cut straight down, sliding the knife out beneath 6:00 (without raising the knife). then cut across the cake from 9:00 to 3:00, using a gentle sawing motion. cut each of these quarters in half, then in half again. this will equal 16 even slices.

3b. rectangular cakes: cut across the width of the cake first, making parallel slices 2 inches apart. then cut down the length of the cake, every 2 inches, across the first set of slices.

---

[5] traditionally, cake slices are 1-by-2-inch slivers, but we prefer heartier 2-by-2-inch squares.

WHAT'S IN MY PANTRY AT ALL TIMES

RECIPES TO TRY AND TO REPEAT

RECIPES TO TRY AND TO REPEAT

RECIPES TO TRY AND TO REPEAT

MENU DIARY

DATE: ....

OCCASION: ....

MEAL:

MENU DIARY

DATE: ....

OCCASION: ....

MEAL:

she savo

conv

sweet ge

cheesy

& just

rs spicy
ersation,
stures,
toasts
desserts.

ners

mind them, modernly.

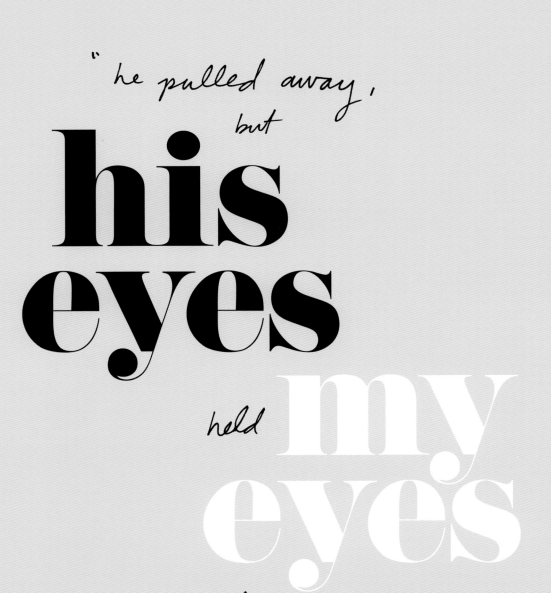

" *he pulled away,* but

his eyes

held **my**

eyes

like hands."

MIRANDA JULY,
no one belongs here more than you

a is for
art of flirtation

despite the number of articles written on the topic, flirting isn't rocket science, thankfully. relax. be your happiest self, make eye contact and employ one of these opening lines:

"hello, stranger." declare it at a friend's party with the cocky irreverence of alice in the film *closer.*

"what are you drinking?" and if his glass is empty, it's a good segue to go to the bar together.

"is this seat taken?" who says you can't win someone over while wining and dining, riding the subway uptown or enjoying a concert?

"where did you get that _____?" fill in the blank with anything—dumpling, cocktail, even the sweater he's wearing. it really doesn't matter.

- chocolate babka

- beautifully packaged french soaps (the kind you get at boutique drugstores)

- a bottle of rosé champagne, st-germain or artisanal lemonade

- a vintage copy of elsa schiaparelli's *shocking life,* f. scott fitzgerald's *the great gatsby, i married adventure* by osa johnson, *beaton in the sixties* or patti smith's *just kids*

- elevated versions of everyday basics: olive oil, balsamic vinegar and the like

- a chic cake stand or plate piled with local treats (ours would include a scrumptious mille crêpe cake from lady m or a batch of frosted sugar cookies by meli & angi)

- a deck of gilded playing cards

- if you love to cook, a special homemade dessert or canned delight (jam, mole verde, sriracha, tomato sauce) with ingredients from your local market

b is for

better-late-than-never gifts

should someone treat you to a present for any reciprocal-gifting holiday[1] when you're least expecting it, the same rules apply whether your delivery is early, on time or ten days late:

respond with a well-composed, handwritten thank-you card to anyone you wouldn't normally have given a gift.

if it's a nearest and dearest you *would* get one for, by all means still do. gifts should be thoughtful, or at least appear not to be the afterthought they were, so if you can't find something to give them or don't have the time, treat them to an experience like a lingering lunch or a rousing round of cocktails, or get tickets for a concert or whatever else you two might fancy doing together.

alternatively, draw up a pretty and witty IOU to explain that you're still looking for the perfect item.

---

[1] if you have forgotten to get someone close a gift for any sort of nonreciprocal-gifting holiday (their birthday, for instance), immediately select one or more of these ideas at right and add one very nice handwritten note about what a wonderful person they are and what a narcissist you are for not remembering.

POP
FIZZ
CLINK

CUVÉE ROSÉ BRUT

1993

chilled pearls

drink divine

tools for remembering:

• a little black book of important dates or perpetual calendar

• your smartphone calendar. set an alarm for two weeks prior to each important date so you have time to get a gift.

• a handwritten list pinned to your refrigerator

ONLY 7% OF ALL COMMUNICATION IS THE WORDS THEMSELVES.

text

THIS MEANS THAT VIA TEXT AND E-MAIL, YOU LOSE SOME HANDY SENSORY CUES:

me?

BODY LANGUAGE (70%) AND VOICE INFLECTION (23%).

c is for

conversational texting

texts, at their heart, are short, sweet, definitely informal, perhaps funny and possibly mundane. they require either no response:

- be aware of your tone before you press send. "please," "thank you" and complete sentences go a long way to soften any message. never text when you're angry or when you've had tee many martoonis. you will regret it later.

- avoid texting under the table during a meeting or meal. the screen may be hidden, but your eyes-down, hunched-over posture and distracting tap-tap-tapping are not.

- and if you have the misfortune of coming across a habitual (and habitually rude) texter, excuse yourself—to the ladies' room, the mahogany bar, another conversation—until they have wrapped it up.

or very clear-cut ones:

they are a prelude or prologue, not a conversation itself. thoughts that need finessing or a subtle touch should be expressed in person or on a phone call; formal matters should be typewritten. if you find yourself sending texts that are paragraphs long, write an e-mail. similarly, continue anything longer than six exchanges by telephone or e-mail.

"when people you greatly admire appear to be thinking deep thoughts, they are probably thinking about

lunc

☐ as soon as possible,
toss leftover food and
wrappers in the kitchen
wastebasket instead of the
tiny under-the-desk bin.

☐ wash your hands.

☐ use a small mirror
to give lips and teeth
a quick once-over.

☐ reapply lipstick.

☐ breeze over nearby
work surfaces with
a disinfectant wipe.

☐ pop a mint.

✳

if you're scheduling
a working lunch for a group,
title your calendar invite
accordingly. elicit sugges-
tions from those attending
about where to order and
pick one. the day before the
event, e-mail the menu from
the chosen restaurant to the
group and take their orders.
as the meeting organizer,
when delivery arrives,
this one's on you.
(or your corporate card.)

d is for
desktop dining

on particularly harried days when even taking your
work outside for a brisk stroll and a café BLT isn't
an option, the short on the cubicle nibble is:

nothing slurpy. nothing overly crunchy. nothing
pungent. that means skip the garlic, onion, chili,
curry, kimchi, popcorn, fish and anything with
a side of bacon.

and the long:

time your meal to the standard lunch hour—you're
less likely to irk your officemates or rattle the hum
of business.

keep a pair of good-looking salt and pepper shakers at
your desk. a packet of nice paper napkins, too. (chances
are you will, in turn, become very popular. the affliction
of moist paper pepper packets is pretty democratic.)

clear some space. move computer accessories, paper-
work and phones out of the way to prevent crumbs
in the keyboard and spills on the spreadsheet.

eat slowly—it's better for you and those around you.

be prepared for interruptions.

h.

DOUGLAS ADAMS

exiting a taxi* gracefully

*or the backseat of a car and, minus step two, booth seating in restaurants.

---

step 1. slide to the very edge of the seat—the edge nearest the car door.

step 2. open the car door.

step 3. keeping your legs together, swing both legs out and place your feet on the ground.

step 4. stand up.

f is for
faux pas fixes

you may be relieved to hear that during general conversation, your little slipups stand out to you more than to anyone else. it's what psychologists call the spotlight effect: a person believes they're in the spotlight but *everyone* thinks they're in the spotlight and so, therefore, no one actually is. that's not because the world is full of narcissists, but rather that our general attention span is shorter and busy multitasking. people will probably notice you said "spank" instead of "thank," but they will also move on.

but should you flub in front of an important and captive audience—a potential employer, your significant other's parents—then that does require a finessed address:

your joke falls flat. turn the silence into a punchline with a witty one-liner ("and that's why i didn't become a comedienne") and move on to another topic.

you constructively criticize your employer's project. turn it into a positive rather than retract your opinion.

you say "spank," not "thank." caffeine is a universal language: your lack of lip coordination is due to a lack of coffee.

you express disdain for someone else's hobby. explain that you're biased—maybe you twisted your ankle playing running charades. that doesn't mean the game isn't enjoyable for everyone.

you talk loudly in a moment of silence. shhhh.

you giggle during a solemn moment of silence. close the giggle loop[2]: disguise it in a cough and excuse yourself.

[2] giggle loop: an exponentially irresistible urge to laugh in inappropriate situations. the more you resist, the funnier the idea of what might have happened had you laughed becomes, resulting in an even stronger desire to laugh. coined by the british in the early 2000s.

i still go to a party
and say something embarrassing
to someone, and then write
them a weird e-mail about it the
next day, and then write them
a text because i think they didn't
get the e-mail. no matter what
happens with your level of success,
you still have to deal with
the baggage that is yourself.

LENA DUNHAM

gifting up, down, all-around

conventional wisdom would have it that, in the office, gifts should "trickle down" from the boss rather than "trickle up" to them. we disagree.

modern work life is hardly conventional: our coworkers are an increasingly important part of our social and emotional lives as we spend more time and energy on the job. as the lines between office and after-hours, weekdays and weekends blur, they're like an extended family. depending how formal your office is, your relationships may be more like what you have with your great-grandmother than your sister.

traditional wisdom also belies the very reason for gifting in the first place: to surprise and delight the other person.

use the holidays or a birthday as an excuse to give your superior something he or she would love that might feel random to wrap up any other time of year: an excellent book, monogrammed stationery, a loaf of your signature homemade banana bread, a vintage vase for the corner of her desk. unless it's something they've specifically mentioned, stick to classic reading, electronics (an artfully designed portable phone charger for top-ups during meetings, for instance), food, wine or office accessories.

gifts for a department at large and for those you interact with in other departments, too should be equally thoughtful, though more democratic. it's logistically— and politically—easier to buy something in bulk. in these cases, think of simple little luxuries people may not normally indulge in themselves.

for the group:

- bottles of artisanal lemonade
- rosé champagne
- early editions of classic books
  with beautiful covers —
  - novels
  - biographies
  - coffee-table tomes
  (find one and then order multiples online)
- cozy cashmere house socks
- sets of clever notecards

for the boss:

- pool resources
  so no one is singled out
  (and the boss gets a fancier gift.)
- a heartfelt note
  (bosses tend to give — not get — so hearing
  how much you appreciate them will make their day.)

wit has tr

wise-c

is

calisthe

with

uth in it;
racking simply
nics words.

DOROTHY PARKER

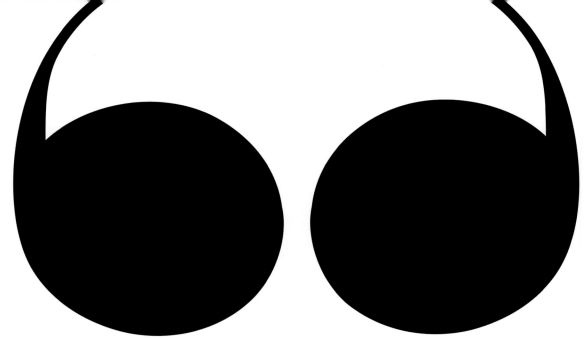

the eye is the window of the soul, the mouth the door.

HIRAM POWERS*

*hiram powers was a leading neoclassical sculptor of the mid-nineteenth century with a thriving business in portraiture and parlor busts, and a passion for creating life-sized, full-figure ideal subjects. his piece greek slave inspired a sonnet by elizabeth barrett browning. his works are held at the smithsonian american art museum, the yale university art gallery, the metropolitan museum of art and, among many others, in the white house collection.

h is for

hello, your name is...?

you make eye contact with someone. their face lights
up with recognition. yours flashes confusion. you've got
three elegant options.

1

in the moment, honesty is the best policy: graciously
acknowledge that you remember meeting the person
and that your memory has temporarily lapsed. (blame
your senior moment on any number of modern-day
calamities.) if you do happen to remember a detail
from that first conversation, mention it at this time:

*"you know, i'm sure we met at amy's christmas party.
you were wearing a beautiful shade of red lipstick.
but i'm drawing a blank on your name."*

2

enlist the help of a quick-witted (and nearby) friend:

*"eloise, i can't remember the name of the woman approaching
us. mind introducing yourself first?"*

3

exclaim a catchall greeting upon meeting:

"hey there." (reserve "darling!" for those you do actually
know.)

and

get into the habit of saying "it's nice to see you" instead
of "it's nice to meet you." it's a handy phrase to have
naturally rolling off your tongue no matter where you
find yourself, who you're with, if you're meeting said
person for the first time or seeing them for the sixth.
because if you can't remember if you've crossed paths
before, it's best to elegantly act as if you, in fact, have.

refreshing your memory

- listen. quite often
  we don't remember
  because we're not
  paying attention.

- repeat the person's name
  back early in conversa-
  tion. ("hello, jane.")

- use a mnemonic device:
  mentally break a difficult
  name up into real
  words with the same
  syllabic cadence.

  saoirse ronan =
  SEER-sha ROH-nin =
  sure she's roman.

instagram at the table

when is the appropriate time to photograph, frame, filter and share your meal when in the company of others (beyond your very best friends who both understand you and would forgive you for anything)?

NEVER.

should you choose to do it anyway, make a to-do of it: announce to the group the gorgeous display before you and that you're going to take a photo.

"

when i ask to photograph someone,
it is because i love
the way they look
and i think i make that clear.
i'm paying them
a tremendous compliment.
What i'm saying is,
i want to take you home with me
and look at you
for the rest of my life.

"

AMY ARBUS

j is for

just a top-up. x 10

in the spirit and commotion of open-bar cocktail parties and festive work events, it's easy to lose track of how many times you've had your drink refilled.

STICK TO A FORMULA: two vodka tonics tops, for instance, rounded out by club sodas with lime.

AND KNOW YOUR TELL: you begin sending random text messages; you have the urge to tell virtual strangers personal information; reapplying lipstick begins to feel like you're filling in the tiniest paint-by-numbers project.

k is for

kicking up your heels, solo

accepting a party invitation with the notion of going on your own is exciting. oh, the people you'll meet! the conversations you'll have! the outfit you'll wear!

actually showing up to the party alone is another brave matter.

▶ dress to the nines, whatever your interpretation of that is. if you look good, you'll feel good. listen to a playlist of your favorite songs on the walk or drive there.

▶ strike up conversations with a compliment or a question about how the other person knows the hostess.

▶ instead of hovering around your hostess all evening, engage with the people around her. ask her if there's anyone particularly interesting you should seek out.

▶ and while it's tempting to be on your phone, put it away. chances are there's someone else looking to start a conversation, too, and they're much more likely to start it with someone who isn't overtly being anti-social.

l is for
lipstick & cloth napkins

of course one can't be certain, but we imagine liz taylor, marilyn monroe, taylor swift, audrey hepburn, lauren bacall and every other confidently lacquered beauty we admire knicking a tissue or paper napkin and blotting their lipstick so as not to leave half-moon marks on the glasses or smudges on the napkins at their tinseltown dinners. that's what we do, at least, at our local bistro and friends' houses.

queen elizabeth II
commissioned her own
lipstick shade,
a soft red-blue, to
match her coronation
robes at the
1952 ceremony.
it was dubbed "the
balmoral lipstick,"
in honor of her scottish
country home.

m is for
madam social butterfly

TWEETS are designed to entertain followers and spark conversation. they also have a habit of going viral, so never tweet anything that you wouldn't say to a crowd of people at a party. if you're stuck for something to talk about but want to have a twitter presence, take on what journalists would call a "beat"—in-depth reporting on a particular topic you find interesting. post a daily inspirational quote by your favorite writers or style icons. inspire your followers to do something new every day with a "today's the day to…" idea. start a twitter book club. keep your content simple, interesting and inspiring.

use **INSTAGRAM** to show off the unique way you see the world, and even make it a more inspiring place. daily selfies and an hour-by-hour documentation of your day are not required.

likewise, when it comes to **FACEBOOK,** exercise caution. set your profile to private. avoid posting unflattering pictures or writing overly personal information on someone else's wall. ask before friending a close friend's ex.

respect others' (and your own) privacy, and remember, whatever you post or comment on online—anywhere, in any medium—will remain in the social sphere long, long after the moment is over. employ the golden rule, don't constantly brag or complain, ignore mean comments and don't fuel argumentative fires.

be an outstanding member of your social circle.

" i've learned that
people will forget what you said,
people will forget what you did,
but people will never forget
how you made them feel. "

MAYA ANGELOU

n is for

neighbors & noise
(theirs. yours.)

---

whether it's in a brooklyn brownstone or a chicago condominium, we prefer apartment living to look and feel more like *pillow talk* and less like *melrose place*— communally festive, architecturally interesting and not a lot of drama.

as urban nomads, we honor more than a few unofficial tenant policies:

▶ weeknight get-togethers mean eight people, max.

▶ rugs are a must on old hardwood floors; heels and boots are not.

▶ vacuuming, lawn-mowing and picture-hanging should be done after nine a.m. and before nine p.m.

▶ prior to weekend soirées, notify each neighbor of the event with a bottle of wine and earplugs. if you like your neighbors, extend an invitation to stop by. if you don't like your neighbors, extend an invitation to stop by. (it's unlikely they'll show, and you win for good manners.)

▶ that said, lower the music when it chimes eleven thirty p.m.

▶ keep it down when entering and exiting the building. be light-footed in stairwells and mindful of shared doors.

while you're at it, be an actively nice neighbor in general. sign for packages, hold open doors, bring newspapers in from the rain, sweep fall leaves from the sidewalk or stoop. welcome new neighbors with a list of your favorite essentials in the area (thai takeout, a wifi-ready café, reputable dry cleaners, a pristine nail salon). include your own number, too. and then sweeten the exchange with some cookies.

it's a salve that will serve you well when you need a little neighborly forgiveness or lock yourself out of your home or the building. it's also a preemptive strategy for when you find yourself dealing with less-than-neighborly behavior.

when that happens, talk to your neighbors first. they may not know how loud they're being. suggest a plan. ask politely for your neighbors to keep it down when it's late, or to shift their activities (like singing) to an earlier time. remember that people are allowed to make noise during the day and into the evening. where evening turns into afterhours is admittedly subjective, but hopefully you're both reasonable people who just want to enjoy your respective evenings, and the problem is solved.

if the noise is keeping you awake at night, chances are you don't really want to get dressed and walk next door. you want to be sleeping. in apartment buildings, the quickest solve may be to knock on the wall where the noise is coming from, to demonstrate that sound does, in fact, travel. if you're friendly enough with your neighbors that you have one anothers' numbers, a polite text can also do the trick. it's better than leaving a note on the door, which may come across as passive-aggressive.

when you can't manage the situation yourself, that's where your building management comes in. noise restrictions are often built into lease agreements, so a note from your landlord will remind the offending neighbor that they're breaking their lease agreement. more often than not, that's the winning argument.

"it's useful being **top** banana in the **shoc**[department.]

department."

HOLLY GOLIGHTLY,
breakfast at tiffany's (1961)

o is for
opinions

have you ever met an interesting or highly respectable person who didn't have an opinion about anything?

(we'll take that as a no.)

say what you think, always. so long as you're thoughtful and say it constructively, you will never go wrong.

if you're asked in a job interview or by your current boss what you think of a project, be forthcoming: you may be the only candidate who wasn't afraid to give a genuine answer. if you're among strangers at a dinner table and you're put on the spot, what you say in response can make you a standout guest. while other ladies may flip their hair and smile silently at the handsome stranger, your flirty banter will be what makes him smile after the party's over.

being the most memorable person in the room has its advantages.

by the same token, if you don't feel compelled any which way about a topic, explain why you don't. that's an opinion, too.

"TO ME, BOSSY IS NOT A PEJORATIVE TERM AT ALL. IT MEANS SOMEBODY'S PASSIONATE AND ENGAGED AND AMBITIOUS AND DOESN'T MIND LEADING." *amy poehler*

REGGIE:

*"do you know
what's wrong
with you?"*

PETER:

" no, what ?"

REGGIE:

"nothing."

AUDREY HEPBURN TO CARY GRANT,

charade (1963)

paying a compliment

don't underestimate the unspoken power of a well-timed compliment. a little poetic praise can break the ice or the tension, or reinforce positive change. it can provide a springboard for an entire conversation or turn right a talk that has veered unexpectedly left. it can seal a deal, tighten a bond, or open the door to something (and someone) new. it can also, more classically, turn a frown upside down.

kind words mean you noticed. people like to be noticed. therefore, don't be shy about giving them, but do be...

GENUINE. on some occasions you may need to pull a compliment out of your back pocket. when you do, don't flatter the person. flattery is insincere, superfluous and strangely needy. instead, pick the first, most striking thing about them—her adventurously red lipstick, his infectious laugh, their piercing blue eyes or eye-catching shoes. most likely it will, by default, be something they take great pride in or have a story about.

SPECIFIC. rather than "great job today," try "your Q4 report was so insightful!" "that cake was dangerously good!" instead of "you're a good cook."

PERSONAL. by this we don't mean pressing a colleague for details on what you think is his or her amazing botox work, but rather adding a personal touch. rather than "you look lovely today," try "i'm so inspired by this blazer situation that i want to go find one myself."

UNEXPECTED. four years ago, during a lively tapas dinner in chelsea, we were given the business card of a new friend. the front was quite (handsomely) standard, but on the back were the typewritten words "i loved your..." followed by the newly handwritten "story of getting locked in at the MoMA!" *that's* a genuine, specific, personal, well-timed compliment.

quite the impression

whether you're meeting a new client or the parents, going on a job interview or along as a friend's plus-one to a dinner party, a great first impression is key. (each does only happen once in a lifetime.)

the nice thing is that there are no specific and hard-to-remember rules. put some conversational etiquette to use and then be yourself. genuine and real is always more memorable than correct.

1. make eye contact.

2. smile.

3. offer a confident handshake. (no wet noodles, please.)

4. ask the other person a question about themselves.

5. use their name in conversation. (incidentally, this will also help you remember it.)

6. look interested: a sudden head tilt, an eyebrow lift or a smile are all subtle signs that you're vested in the conversation.

7. if the situation lends itself, compliment them.

8. be gracious. at the end of the conversation (or to make a quick-but-polite exit), say thank you and that it was lovely to see them.

...because I see her standing,
with her black velvet slacks,
hands-a-pockets, thin, slouched,
cig hanging from her lips,
the smoke itself curling up,
her little black back hairs of
short haircut combed down fine + sleek
her lipstick, pale brown skin,
dark eyes, the way shadows play
on her high cheekbones, the nose,
the little soft shape of chin to neck,
the little adam's apple,
so hip, so cool, so beautiful,
so modern, so new ...

JACK KEROUAC'S DESCRIPTION OF MARDOU FOX IN *the subterraneans the biggest compliment for me is when young women*

tell me

i've inspired them and their work.

ANH DUONG

r is for

returning the compliment

---

say thank you, even if you feel your presentation could have gone smoother or that your outfit leaves lots to be desired. rejecting someone's good words implies that they have no taste, and sucks that delicious positivity straight out of the air.

you won't come across as phony if you answer a compliment with a genuine compliment, either, though you're not obliged to do so. telling the person, "that is so sweet of you to say" is an accolade in and of itself.

starting and stopping small talk

keeping in mind that everyone at the party is there to meet new people (if they weren't, they would have stayed at home)...

▸ wait for an opening in the conversation, then introduce yourself to the group or a person in it. if you know someone, a little tap on their shoulder or a eyebrow raise is all it'll take for them to make room for you.

▸ jumping into someone else's conversation only works if you're sitting directly next to them.

▸ the easiest conversation to join is one with one other person.

▸ when it's time to employ an exit strategy, discreetly bow out of a larger group with an "excuse me." if you're talking to one other person and don't want to leave them stranded, walk them over to another group or include someone new in yours. once the conversation is in full swing, you can politely leave them.

▸ the person with the higher status (your boss, for example) generally dictates how long the conversation will go, so continue the conversation until they do the above or something similar to you.

▸ one easy way to tell if you've overstayed your verbal welcome is if the other person's eyes begin wandering the room. and wandering...and wandering...

"
intima
I LIKE LARGE PARTIES. THEY'RE SO

AT SMALL PARTIES THERE ISN'T ANY

privac

"

JORDAN BAKER,
the great gatsby

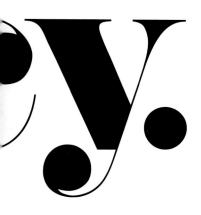

to plus-one or not to plus-one?

more is always merrier, right? not quite.

for large parties, it's probably okay to arrive with an unannounced friend, though it's better to pop a quick e-mail to the hostess beforehand, expressing your excitement at the impending merrymaking and mentioning your guest.

for seated dinners, weddings and anything requiring a reservation or tickets, the awkwardness it would cause for your hostess outweighs any it causes for you. don't do it.

while a sidekick is always comfortable, never hesitate to go solo—you never know whom you'll meet, which makes the whole affair that much more thrilling.

✳ a note to hostesses:
if budget and space allows, indicate that your invitation is meant for two by addressing it to "jane smith and guest." or if your guest is coupled, find out the spelling of her significant other's name and list both on the invitation.

and if it isn't, revisit our favorite cheeky line, "for your lovely eyes only." (it sounds so much nicer than "no plus-ones allowed.")

steal *the* spot

t is also for

there are three types of exits, but only one entrance

the exits

in small gatherings (fewer than fourteen), engage your host before departing. find your coat, make your embraces, pay your compliments.

if it's a midsize event and your calendar calls for an early departure, mention it in your RSVP. or if your mood changes en route, tell your hostess "i can only stay for twenty minutes but i so wanted to see you!" when greeting them. no one will notice if you change your mind yet again and stay longer.

larger affairs afford more wiggle room. we like making a french exit,[3] wherein you quietly duck out *sans* farewell.

the keys to a successful french exit: say hello to the hostess upon arrival and then e-mail her first thing the next day (or call at a kind hour) with your gratitude and to swap juicy anecdotes from the evening.

the entrance

take a moment to pause and survey the room. (to be dazzling is to be approachable and relaxed.) proceed to do a lap, elegantly making your way to the hostess to say thank you while keeping your right hand free for handshakes and half-hugs, and only then making your way to the bar.[4]

this should be done somewhere between five and fifteen minutes after the invitation time.

[3] it's also called the irish good-bye and the dutch leave. clearly it's a popular tactic.
[4] memorable entrances can also, of course, be unplanned. when nan kempner was turned away at la côte basque on east 55th street in the 1960s because she was wearing a pantsuit, she wriggled out of her trousers without missing a beat and entered the restaurant wearing only the top half of the outfit—an yves saint laurent tunic-turned-minidress.

u is for

u-turning
a conversation

braggarts, bulldozers and bores. name-droppers, narcissists and know-it-alls. ramblers, whiners and gossips. here's a wonderful, wily way to redirect a conversation with any of these types.

1

let them talk for a minute or two. acknowledge the offending topic or attitude: *"understood." "i see where you're coming from."*

2

immediately and gracefully maneuver the dialogue onto a more positive course, redirect their attention to something within the environment, drop a disarming compliment or evoke an element of surprise. *"speaking of…" "that reminds me…" "incidentally…" "before i forget…" "i've been meaning to tell you…" "i'm curious what you think about…" "have you heard about…?"*

3

if that fails, wrap up the conversation and politely excuse yourself. no apologies necessary.

"OBJECTIVITY DOESN'T MEAN TREATING ALL SIDES EQUALLY. IT MEANS GIVING EACH SIDE A HEARING." *christiane amanpour*

v is for
very much, thank you

---

expressing your gratitude doesn't always need to be a formal affair now that texts and e-mails have become socially polite. whatever your medium, sending it sooner is best (three days or less), but better late than never. you may need to be clever with what you write, but there's no need to belabor its tardiness. concentrate on the gift itself and, of course, be sincere. it will still mean a lot that you made the effort.

the text
an off-the-cuff message best sent to close friends and family within a few hours of said act of kindness, and love interests after fun dates. swap your "dear" and "kindly" for a witty emoji, and avoid mucking up your appreciation with careless misspellings and—OMG, no!—digital slang.

the e-mail
a note well-suited for day-after reminiscences, with writing space for a few more details and anecdotes. these are also especially useful to send after a job interview as long as you avoid any "copy and paste"-style language, and still send a physical thank-you note after.

the handwritten note

our preferred method[5] for wedding, birthday and shower gifts, presents from close relatives and our boss.

here, err on the side of proper. that being said, you also want to sound like yourself.

use "mr." "mrs." or "ms." for anyone you're on a last-name basis with. for close friends and family, you can call them whatever name or term of endearment you use—if you call your granny "bubbles," start your card to her with that.

write naturally. composing the note in your head first helps to keep it conversational and not too stiff. use contractions ("i'm so glad!" instead of "i am so glad!") unless you're specifically drawing attention to that statement. type or write it out to organize your thoughts and check spelling before putting pen to fancy paper.

refer to the actual gift, event or even conversation you're acknowledging, and then call out something specific about it. do you love the bracelet your friend gave you so much that you've worn it for a week straight? say so!

ways to close a thank-you letter: fondly, warmly, kindly, affectionately, best, yours.

if you've received a really nice thank-you gift from someone—and especially if you're swooning over it— by all means, send a short note back. something to the effect of "the bouquet of flowers/gorgeous candle/ bottle of champagne was so unnecessary to send— but i'm so glad you did!" will make their day.

---

[5] princess diana wrote her thank-you notes each evening before bed.

charlie black:
well, i don't think "preppy" is a very useful term.
i mean, it might be descriptive for someone who is still
in school or college, but it's ridiculous to refer to a man
in his 70s like averell harriman as preppy. and none of the
other terms people use—WASP, P.L.U., et cetera—are of much
use either. and that's why i prefer the term "U.H.B."

nick smith:
what?

charlie black:
U.H.B. it's an acronym for urban haute bourgeoisie.

cynthia mclean:
is our language so impoverished that we have to use
acronyms or french phrases to make ourselves understood?

charlie black:
yes.

nick smith:
U.H.B. the term is brilliant and long overdue.
but it's a bit of a mouthful, isn't it—U.H.B?
wouldn't it be better just to pronounce it simply uhb?

charlie black:
well, i didn't expect it to gain immediate acceptance.

nick smith:
no, no, i think it's a useful term. the fact that
it sounds ridiculous could be part of its appeal.

cynthia mclean:
you see the world from such lofty heights
that everything below is a bit comical to you, isn't it?

nick smith:
[standing up and adjusting his tuxedo lapels]
yes.

CHRIS EIGEMAN, ISABEL GILLIES AND TAYLOR NICHOLS IN *metropolitan (1990)*

witty repartee

banter is like a theater improv scene in real life. it requires spontaneity, quick wit and an element of give-and-take. (did we also mention it's quite good fun?)

assemble a cast. to experience the *pop fizz clink* of good banter, you need at least one willing and able partner in crime—ideally a whole algonquin table[6] of them.

accept information. you don't need to find perfectly common ground: your lack of knowledge on a topic is a fun chance to play devil's advocate; sitting on opposite sides of the fence can prove quite fruitful. we once got into an unexpectedly playfully heated late-night conversation about the grammatical use of colons and semi-colons. the grammar book *eats, shoots & leaves* came into play; so did john f. kennedy's 1961 inaugural address.[7] but what started us down this rabbit hole, we haven't a clue. on that note, have opinions. and facts.

ask questions, listen thoughtfully, make statements. make sure you're adding to the discussion; otherwise it's a game of twenty questions.

humor, yes. sarcasm, no. keep the conversation flowing; don't stop it in its tracks.

get into a good rhythm. subtly mirroring one or two of your fellow conversationalist's gestures, tones or choice of words builds camaraderie and rapport.

then raise the stakes. circling back to our improv metaphor, your plot line should crescendo rather than plateau. hit an awkward pause? bring others into the conversation circle.

don't overthink it. there are no big mistakes here. it's just small talk.

[6] the algonquin round table: a noted group of new york city writers, critics, actors and general wits including dorothy parker and harpo marx who met for lunch each day at the algonquin hotel between 1919 and 1929. also known as the "vicious circle."

[7] the speech has been printed two ways. "and so, my fellow americans: ask not what your country can do for you—ask what you can do for your country."
—official inaugural address transcript, january 20, 1961. vs. "john f. kennedy issued this stirring challenge: 'ask not what your country can do for you; ask what you can do for your country.'" —*the new york times,* 1961.

w is also for
weddings and white

---

of course, the fail-safe answer if you are a guest to a wedding or bridal shower is: don't wear white. but there are a few cases where you may, particularly in summer. we advise erring on the side of reserve—there's a difference between showing up at your best friend's wedding in a floor-length white silk gown and showing up in a dress merely edged in ecru. so if the wedding is more nontraditional and the bride doesn't mind, here are two tips for wedding-guest white:

choose a dress that's only partially white—a white bodice with a flouncy floral skirt, for instance.

wear a dress that has a white background and an allover print in a different color.

xoxo-ing friends and acquaintances

---

one can read the love in the room by the greetings happening within it: formal handshakes, stiff waves, joyous shrills of laughter and hugs. all, clear signs.

the social kiss falls, pleasantly and platonically, somewhere in the middle of this pendulum, which makes it a physical and social minefield. the rules can differ wildly regarding whom to pucker up for, when to lean in, which cheek leads and whether it's a figurative or actual cheek kiss. there is the potential for nose grazes, head bumps and even an inadvertent liplock. what happens at a manhattan art gallery opening may perplex your husband's friends at his high school reunion in another part of the country.

even the french, who invented the social kiss and intrinsically do all things with a certain *savoir faire*, don't have it easy: in their country, the number of pecks can vary from one to five. (on average, it's two in the cities and four in the hinterlands.)

what we do know is this: follow the leader and pick up on social cues, whether at a house party, a business dinner, a bar or a wedding receiving line. if your host or client greets you with extended arms and leans in for a peck, do the same. (right cheek. but be prepared to change direction at the last second.)

if you're unsure, get ahead of the situation: smile widely, nod warmly and extend your hand for a friendly shake to disarm any social kissing shenanigans whatsoever.

kisses by country*

1 united states, canada, philippines and brazil

england, spain, italy + france

2

3 the netherlands, poland, switzerland, belgium, lebanon + france

4 france

*as far as we can figure

y is for

you broke it

accidents happen. when you scratch your hostess' best dylan album, spill wine on her sheepskin rug or shatter her inherited fabergé egg...

fess up and apologize immediately.

if it's beyond repair or irreplaceable, make amends for your bad behavior and send her something really, truly fabulous—box seats to the ballet, a case of excellent wine, a new piece of art, a vintage vase— and a handwritten note. never send cash or a random gift certificate.

if the item can be repaired or replaced with her guidance, gather the pertinent information (manufacturer, retailer, age, material) and snap a picture of the damaged pieces. there are matching services such as replacements ltd. that will identify new and vintage housewares—china, crystal, silver, collectibles—for free.

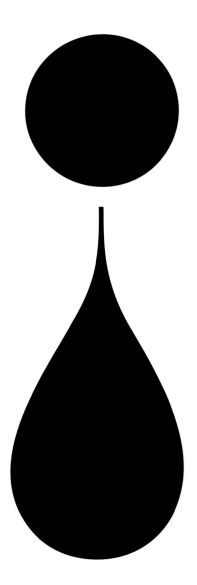

troves for replacement treasures

- 1stdibs.com
- ebay.com
- jaysonhome.com
  (the flea section)
- etsy.com
- chairish.com
- thehighboy.com

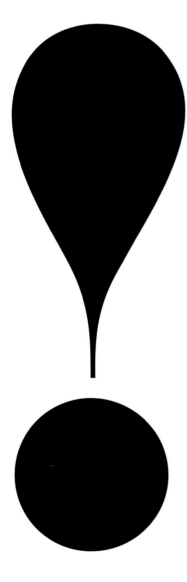

z is for
zingers for a dull date

one would think the kindest thing to do is tough it out, but that doesn't do either of you any favors. you'll both have wasted an evening that you'll never, ever get back.

plus, some people simply aren't savvy enough to know when someone's just not into them. this is when a third wheel comes in quite handy. plan to have a friend telephone you thirty minutes into your *tête-à-tête* with some plausible reason you need to leave immediately. if he's creepy, excuse yourself and go. if there are simply no sparks, genuinely apologize to mr. not-right, tell him it was so nice to meet him and let him walk you out of the venue.

GIFTS I LOVE TO GIVE...

...AND GET

MY SECRET GIFT RESOURCES

IMPORTANT DATES TO REMEMBER

her e-mail
but she
remem
to
grand

ls pile up
always
bers
call her
mother.

style

it's more than the stuff that surrounds you.

"have nothing
in your houses
that you do not
know to be

useful

or believe to be

beau

no one "decorates" their home. (or themselves for that matter.) they embark on an expedition.

the choices you make are a journey that tells the story of you. and so, even before you string up the fairy lights, decorate the table or pop the champagne, your home should already be the best expression of yourself.

that doesn't mean having lots of expensive things, or the "right" things, or the things you think you need to own because you're grown-up.

your most valuable asset is your imagination, and your home should feel well-loved and lived-in. treasure every square foot of it and make every nook and cranny come alive with pieces accumulated, incorporated and showcased over time that have fond memories and stories to tell.

surround yourself with the things you love. discard the rest.

WILLIAM MORRIS

ingrid-isms

spend fifteen minutes on the phone with brooklyn-based interiors writer ingrid abramovitch and you'll glean enough decorating advice and insight to spruce up multiple abodes. here are some of our favorites:

66

new yorkers have to constantly edit— their wardrobe, their furniture— which makes them take a careful look at what they own, what means the most. space is finite, so everything has to be beautiful or functional.

any self-respecting
new yorker isn't getting
all their furniture from
a single store.
people want personality:
one-of-a-kind pieces,
handmade pieces, vintage pieces.
they don't want their
apartments to look like
anybody else's.

you might not
have floor space, but
everyone has walls!

show and tell

flea markets, estate sales, thrift shops, auction houses, vintage bookshops and grandma's attic are treasure troves for discovering new loves or adding to existing ideas.

here are four ways to collect your thoughts...

MATERIAL
▸ sterling-silver flatware in different patterns
▸ decorative mirrors
▸ vintage hotel silver serving pieces and utensils
▸ lacquered or mirrored trays

COLOR
▸ stock glass-fronted cabinets with assorted platters, plates and bowls in the same color. (ours would be in maraschino red.)
▸ completely unrelated shelf trinkets in the same hue
▸ a compilation of colored glass bottles or jars to create a windowsill garden

ERA
▸ select a particularly inspiring era (say, the art deco movement of the 1920s) and amass a bricolage of ashtrays, vases and other accessories to sprinkle throughout a room.

MOTIF
▸ all things emblazoned with a sly red fox—paper-weight, pen cup, letter opener—placed on a tray to fancy up a corner of your desk
▸ artful, practical tchotchkes (like conversational salt and pepper shakers)
▸ patterned tiles picked up on a far-flung adventure as a backsplash in the kitchen

tchotchke
(chahch-key)

noun:
a small object that is both decorative and functional, derived from the slavic word for "trinket." also called a knickknack.

"CAN ONE DESIRE TOO MUCH OF A GOOD THING?" *william shakespeare,* as you like it

...and some clever ways to display them

BIG STATEMENT VS. SMALL TALK

line a hall, stairway or other narrow passage with mirrors of all sizes and frames accumulated from flea markets and road trips. (DIY versailles!)	use vintage china pieces from the dining table for anything you'd otherwise use a small dish for: to hold candy, your keys, even desk supplies.
perch a glamorous and beloved pair of heels, a vintage tea pot, a stack of plates or other pretty object under a bell jar on a credenza.	hang shelves equidistant the length of a curtainless window with a less-than-scenic view and prop with glass perfume bottles from around the world or passed down from your grandmother.
extend the windowsills in a study or playroom with hanging shelves and line with storybooks for a kid-level library.	repurpose glass jars as destination-specific time capsules, filling them with photobooth strips, matchbooks, loose foreign change and other travel tidbits after each trip.
have your favorite word or phrase written in neon lights on a plain white wall.	toss decorative matchbooks in a glass jar.
hang a collection of chandeliers in unexpected places, such as the back porch and the garage.	replace standard doorknobs with indulgent midcentury ones picked up in palm springs.
strip, paint or reupholster inherited furniture.	tuck a needlepoint pillow emblazoned with your catchphrase into the corner of a wingback.

the art of the salon wall

a salon wall is our celebrated way to display a highly personal, visually interesting mix of art and pieces that suddenly become art once they're cleverly arranged in a creative montage.

our tricks

▶ pick an aesthetic—as opposed to a specific theme—to encourage cohesive variety. (we veer toward clean lines with touches of vintage and metallic.)
▶ play around with different pieces to find the right ratio of everyday objects to art. we love the modern mix of an illustration, a painting (oil or watercolor), a photograph, one or two pieces of typography, a book cover, a handful of prints and something totally random—like a playing card affixed to the wall with a pushpin.
▶ keep the color of the wall in mind. a print that contains accents of the same hue helps pull it all together.
▶ choose one or two pieces to put in mats.
▶ multiples of the same frame lend a sense of order; a hodgepodge mix feels more nonchalantly tossed together. (we like a combination of black, white, wooden and brass—and something unframed.)

our hang up

no. 1 measure the display wall.
no. 2 find your sweet spot: the center of a group of paintings and photographs should be $5\frac{1}{2}$ feet from the floor. (that's eye level for most people.)
no. 3 using masking tape, map the dimensions of the wall on an empty floor space.
no. 4 arrange your selected objects, framed, within the tape lines on the floor until the desired look is achieved.
no. 5 take a photo of the floor arrangement and begin hanging the items.
no. 6 use a level to check that the frames are straight.
no. 7 step back and admire your work.

gestalt:
(geh SHtält)

noun:
1. a german word meaning "form" or "shape."
2. in other languages, an organized whole that is perceived as greater than the sum of its parts.

expected

- photographs
- magazine tears
- paintings
- mirrors
- postcards
- illustrations

unexpected

- a wall clock
- a piece of a map
- album covers
- elaborate drawer pulls in a shadowbox frame
- books with beautiful covers
- vintage tourism ads, all from a single destination
- our favorite sayings
- a page of sheet music
- beloved (or very expensive) wallpaper swatches

"BUY THE BEST AND YOU ONLY CRY ONCE." *ancient chinese proverb*

come to your five senses

layer at least one complementary element from
each category in a room
to create a comfortable
nest for guests.

scent

▸ use a candle[1] as you
would perfume: bold
enough to be noticed,
but not overpowering.
▸ spritz linen spray
in the guest room.
▸ hook sachets onto
hangers in the coat closet.
▸ light subtly sophisticated
japanese or french incense
on the perimeter of
a patio.
▸ simmer a mix of spices,
herbs and fruits on the
kitchen stovetop: oranges
and cloves in winter,
lemons and rosemary at
summer's end. (or go the
more traditional route
and bake cookies.)
▸ leave a container of
ground coffee or a jar
with a couple of cotton
balls soaked in vanilla
open on a shelf in your
refrigerator door.
▸ hang a couple of
eucalyptus sprigs at the
far edge of the shower.
▸ add a few drops of
essential oils to your
lamps' lightbulbs.
▸ fresh flowers[2]

taste

▸ set a fancy tin of individually wrapped mints
in the powder room;
footed dishes of butter-
scotch hard candies in
the den; cucumber water
on the kitchen counter.
▸ introduce out-of-town
houseguests to a plate
of local specialties.
▸ arrange a make-your-
own drink tray.
▸ keep an organized binder
of menus of the best
neighborhood takeout.

[1] find scent-spiration on your travels.
we've inquired on more than one
occasion about the specific aroma
of a hotel lobby. (and sometimes they're
even sold in the hotel gift shop.)
[2] fragrant flowers are, on average, pricey
flowers. buy a stem or two and place
them in a bud vase in a strategic place,
like the edge of a powder room sink.
we love lilac, freesia, gardenias and
casablanca lilies. befriending a green-
thumbed neighbor who excels at
honeysuckle, jasmine and japanese
wisteria might also earn you a clipping
now and then.

nice accent

use pops of these hues to create a mood

red: decadent.

orange: energizing.

green: relaxing.

yellow: cheerful. encourages conversation.

blues: calming and dreamy. (maybe that's why it's the world's favorite color, according to pantone.)

pink: nurturing.

violet: creative.

masters in painting

• the first step in choosing a color: paint a variety of samples on the wall and take a look at them at different times of the day and in different light before deciding.

• if your plaster isn't perfectly smooth, use an eggshell or semigloss finish.

• store leftover paint in airtight mason jars for touch-ups. you'll be able to spot your color at a glance; plus, the jars are easier to seal than a paint can.

sight

▶ think of paint like lipstick for the room. it's remarkable how a coat of color (like the ones at left) will instantly shift people's mood.

▶ treat lamps like jewelry: choose something statement-making and eclectic. (estate sale finds can be so bad they're good.) try parchment shades, which are softer than stark white, or custom shades made from your great-grandmother's engagement party dress.

▶ wallpaper one accent wall with a bold print to create the feel of a room within a room.

▶ follow one color thread throughout multiple rooms—red-striped curtains in the kitchen, a red ikat tablecloth in the dining room, a red suzani pillow on your bed and red flowers in the entrance hall, for example—to hint at the idea of continuity.

▶ splurge on an expensive, high-drama wallpaper for a tiny space like a powder room; stencil a bathroom wall.

▶ use a favorite fabric to make crisp roman shades and matching pillows.

▶ wallpaper the ceiling.

sound

▶ a vintage record player and a stack of favorite records.

▶ have digital playlists at the ready for a variety of moods.

▶ set an old-school radio alarm clock dial to a classical, public or college radio station in the guest room.

▶ open windows to hear birds chirping.

touch

▶ add tactile variety: place a mirrored side table next to a linen sofa; let velvet fabrics flock with satin and/or metals.

▶ arrange houseplants along a mantel.

▶ a cashmere throw

▶ a silk robe tossed nonchalantly on a bathroom hook

▶ sisal, sheepskin and cowhide rugs

▶ crown wall moldings, wainscoting, beadboard, coffered ceilings and ceiling medallions

PALE PINK **+** BLACK **+** CREAM

SHOCKING PINK **+** NAVY **+** PALE PINK

MARASCHINO RED **+** AQUA **+** GREEN

CITRON **+** GREY **+** BLACK

put out the welcome mat in every room

your entry
this must be the place!

since this is where you welcome guests into your home, it's important to set this area apart and make it almost extra inviting. establish a distinct space with showstopping wallpaper, a daring paint color or black and white stripes that carry over onto the ceiling. brighten up the setting with eye-catching essentials: a sparkly mirror, a poppy red enamel umbrella stand, a patterned tray or vintage toast rack to hold mail, sculptural hooks for keys and coats or a celebratory brass chandelier. still have room? add a bench or slipper chair with a cushion in your favorite color or graphic pattern.

anatomy of an "oh shit" closet
identify a closet that, on any given day, is only partially in use. designate half that closet space to shelving—some lined with large, empty baskets, others left bare—so you have room to throw unsightly messes, chores, unmentionables and major projects when unexpected guests arrive. if this is your coat closet, arrange the shelving above the hanging rail and below the hems of your coats.

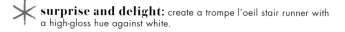 **surprise and delight:** create a trompe l'oeil stair runner with a high-gloss hue against white.

your living room
and how to zone it.

whether you have a studio apartment or a grand salon, there are some golden rules of what to have and what to place where.

▶ two facing sofas with consistent seat heights—or one sofa facing two wingback chairs—around a coffee table encourages interaction.[3] (place them close so people can be heard.)

in small spaces, use two poufs or benches in lieu of the second sofa or chairs.

in large ones, create multiple conversation "nooks" and dot additional clusters of seating—a settee and a chair, two chairs flanking a side table, one large ottoman—around the room.

▶ use furniture of contrasting heights and sizes. the eyes will dance across the room to take it all in, so it automatically makes a space feel dynamic and free spirited. if you have a tall étagère on one wall, place a low chair and side table nearby.

[3] groupings of art and objects subliminally encourage small talk, too: look for single photographs or paintings that contain three or more things; display a collection of candle holders on a credenza rather than one on its own.

10 interesting books for the coffee table:

- *de kooning: an american master*

- *vogue: the covers*

- *flair annual 1953*

- *in the pink: dorothy draper, america's most fabulous decorator*

- *frida kahlo: face to face*

- *slim aarons: once upon a time*

- *places to go, people to see* by kate spade new york

- *domus 1928–1999, volumes 1–12*

- *cecil beaton: the art of the scrapbook*

- *things we love* by kate spade new york

✳

for her apartment on fifth avenue in new york city, babe paley would request multiple plans from decorators and then took elements she liked of each to make something totally different.

▶ to create a private conversation spot in an open space, take arrangement inspiration from the design of an antique conversation chair:[4] place two wingback chairs facing in opposite directions side by side, with a small drink table in between—they should overlap enough that the two sitting there can converse over the table.

▶ have seating that men and women alike will feel comfortable in. if you have a pink satin loveseat, add a stately wingback or club chair; balance a chesterfield sofa with a feminine chaise, bergère or slipper chair.

▶ lighting that makes everyone look amazing is a must: not too bright, not too dark. (dimmers come in quite handy here.) swap out some of your lightbulbs for (highly flattering) pink ones, and vary the height and source of your light: table or floor lamps, candles, overhead chandeliers.

▶ slip in a couple of tiny drink tables.

 surprise and delight: paint the inside of a non-working fireplace. use a vintage ceramic planter (the more conversational, the better) to corral remote controls or assorted cords. have a professional oil painting made of your dog, cat or hedgehog and hang it in a gilded frame.

[4] conversation chair: a double chair wherein two people sit side by side but face in opposite directions.

your kitchen

it's not just where you cook.

---

when you throw a party, most people wind up in the
kitchen. if the thought perplexes you, consider that
a kitchen is both cozy and lively—two elements of
a fun time.

so involve your guests in the preparation, or at least
provide the atmosphere to make them feel like they are:
a bar counter with stools so one or two can chat and
arrange the occasional plate of crudité, for instance.

and make your space as glamorous as it is functional:
install a chandelier; swap out plain cabinet doors
for metal ones; hang a gigantic piece of art on the
wall. keep your washing-up liquid in an elegant glass
decanter.

but don't ever let anyone clean up, no matter how much
they insist. house rule.

✳ **surprise and delight:** paint the inside of your kitchen drawers
lemon yellow. install decorative knobs and plates on utillity doors
(e.g., to the laundry room, basement, pantry).

your dining room

this is perhaps the last room in the house in which it would feel terribly gauche to have a television, and we're thankful for that.

some of our finest, liveliest conversations are had here, when everyone's pushed back from the table, poured another glass of wine and debated ideas around a satellite of crumb-strewn dessert plates.

so we treat it as a parlor rather than a space to dine and dash, with lo-fi diversions around the room's edges: a cozy settee under a window, a telescope in a corner, a baby grand piano for impromptu concerts, a stash of board games, a basket of photo albums or a record player and a crate of LPs.

sometimes—be it space constraints or that we simply love the light coming through the window—we've been inspired to use our dining room as one of these, too:

▶ a handsome library: wrap the walls with bookcases filled with your most prized tomes and quirky gewgaws (a watercolor globe, a marble bust, fox-shaped topiary).

▶ a fanciful, monday-through-friday home office: push the other chairs to the room's perimeter, frame your "desk" with two adjustable task lamps and stash office supplies in the china cabinet. (come weekends, pop your lamps and computer in there, too, and no one will be the wiser.)

▶ a convenient playroom: host art projects around a round table that can be dressed up with a tablecloth for dinner; hide toys and craft supplies away inside a tall hutch. but leave out the knick-knacks that delight the grown-ups, too: a midcentury-style dollhouse, a remote-controlled sports car and a clip-on ping-pong net and paddles.

hiding the rest of it away

- a screened closet or wardrobe

- a brightly painted chest of drawers

- labeled baskets

- trays in all shapes, sizes, shades

- lucite boxes

- vintage candy boxes

- an antique armoire with a glass front to hold shoes and sweaters

- a fuchsia ottoman with hidden storage

your powder room

decorate it as you would any other space: a fresh coat
of paint; a vintage chandelier; embroidered linens;
a zebra-print stool; a mirrored tray dotted with your
favorite perfumes, soaps, bubble bath and glass apothecary jars filled with cotton balls. have a curtain made
from yards of gorgeous fabric. (if you use an outdoor
fabric, you can skip the lining altogether.) hang fluffy,
snowy white towels or vibrant ones.

find a great antique mirror for your powder room. the
slight mottling of vintage glass casts a flattering glow,
and when people feel fabulous, they have more fun.

surprise and delight: cover plain light switches in sheet music,
a graphic pattern fabric or a metallic or mirror cover.

your outdoor space
in three sizes

---

small

LOCATION	balcony, deck, front stoop or fire escape
TOOLKIT	hanging baskets, window boxes, a watering can and a pair of shears
PLANT LIST	all things edible (nasturtiums, calendula, violets), herbal (basil, mint, lemon verbena) and vertiginous (colonnade apple tree, fig tree)
PRETTY TOUCHES	a patterned outdoor rug and a handmade wooden muddler for fresh mojitos and other refreshing garden-to-glass beverages

medium

LOCATION	sunroom, rooftop, courtyard or communal green space—converted into a secret garden
TOOLKIT	trellises, arbors and unexpected planters
PLANT LIST	all things fragrant (wisteria, honeysuckle, morning glories); and feathered (ferns, maiden grass, queen anne's lace)
PRETTY TOUCHES	lounge chairs and patio umbrella in bright and/or graphic stripe linens, glamorously practical malamine serving trays and a birdbath

large

LOCATION	backyard, poolside patio or wide-berthed porch
TOOLKIT	a landscape architect, lawn service and quite possibly a pool attendant
PLANT LIST	flora with serious flair: yucca, hostas, palm trees, perennial hibiscus, delphinium and oriental lilies
PRETTY TOUCHES	outdoor curtains, bocce court, two-person hammock

zhoozh:
(tszuj)

slang; to tweak,
tidy or finesse
(something); to make
more compelling.
commonly used
with "up."

your guest room
imagine it's a room in a boutique hotel.
(your boutique hotel.)

▶ fresh, crisp sheets[5]
▶ a full-length mirror
▶ bedside tables generous enough to handle the essentials, such as a working alarm clock, a reading lamp with adjustable brightness, a water carafe and glass, a stack of interesting reads (vintage novels, local guidebooks, magazines)
▶ artisanal chocolates
▶ a small vase of fresh flowers
▶ extra blankets (one lightweight throw and one heavier duvet)
▶ a candle and box of matches or rosewater room spray
▶ a lowball glass and a nice, new toothbrush
▶ a pair of fresh, cozy, woolen house socks (the kind you'd wear in a rustic cabin) rolled up and tied with a ribbon, baker's twine or a bright elastic to wear and take home

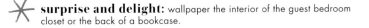 **surprise and delight:** wallpaper the interior of the guest bedroom closet or the back of a bookcase.

[5] good-quality sheets are a necessary indulgence. have two sets of sheets for each bed in complementary designs to mix and match. the glamour is in the details: scallops or piped edges, or a crisp and simple set that's chicly monogrammed. when you use them, iron just the pillowcases and the part of the top sheet that's visible when you fold it over.

interesting designing women *(with interesting lives)*

elsie de wolfe
a.k.a. lady mendl
1859–1950

WHO   an american actress, author and the inventor of interior design as a profession.

WHAT   before elsie, decorating was left to (almost exclusively male) upholsterers and architects. she rebelled against heavy, dark victorian clutter with her signature femininity: pastel paints, french antiques, curvaceous vanities, delicate writing desks, racy animal prints. among her clients were amy vanderbilt, adelaide frick, the duchess of windsor, condé nast and cole porter, who immortalized her in the lyrics of *anything goes.*

WHEN   she penned her influential *the house in good taste* in 1913 but was breaking rules and taking major commissions—homes, private clubs, opera boxes, a dormitory at barnard college—throughout the 1920s and 1930s.

WORDS OF WISDOM   "never complain, never explain."
(she had this embroidered onto taffeta pillows.)

dorothy draper
1889–1969

WHO   an american interior decorator and author.

WHAT   an unapologetic maximalist, she is the progenitor of american baroque: bold colors, rococo scrollwork, stripes abutting florals, flurries of mirrors. there's also her nine-foot birdcage chandelier for the MoMA's dorotheum café and a pink polka-dotted truck for the packard motor car company. her two books—1939's *decorating is fun!* and the 1941 follow-up *entertaining is fun!*—are a treasured part of our library.

she hit her stride in the 1930s, when she redecorated the lobby of manhattan's carlyle hotel, finishing it off with a pendant light modeled after a hot-air balloon. a year later, she rethought a row of houses in the sutton place neighborhood by painting them all black with white trim and colorful front doors. a slew of high-profile hotel projects followed that kept her busy through the 1950s: chicago's drake, washington d.c.'s mayflower, hollywood's arrowhead springs.

"i'll always put in one controversial item. it makes people talk."

sheila bridges
1964–

an american interior decorator, designer, television host and author.

her riffs on decorative arts—such as traditional french toile, from which bridges' designed her harlem toile de jouy wallpaper and fabric—hints both at a very witty eye and to bridges' belief in telling life stories and cultural history through interior decor. a low-maintenance and highly personal aesthetic punctuated with practical advice.

she started her own firm in 1994 and has designed personal residences and public offices with the same visually intelligent eye, including the 8,300-square-foot harlem offices of former president bill clinton and his staff, as well as projects at columbia university and princeton university.

"whether we're dealing with antiques or modern furniture, everything can be classic."

you are the finish-ing touch

"AN EXERCISE IN STYLE IS NOT A SUPERFICIAL MATTER—OUR WHOLE LIVES ARE ALSO AN EXERCISE IN STYLE." *zadie smith*

why don't you
wear a...

• fancy full skirt
and a t-shirt

• trench coat
and a mini dress for
a party outdoors

• fancy dress
and a men's watch

• men's tuxedo
and lavish hair

• oversize white button-up
shirt (sleeves rolled up)
and dazzling jewels

• ball gown
and a unfussy ponytail

"you can have anything you want in life," wrote costume designer **EDITH HEAD** in her book *how to dress for success,* "if you dress for it."

what you want in these three or four hours of your life as a hostess is to experience a bit of splendor at home, landing somewhere on a sliding scale between nonchalant glamour and glamorous nonchalance.

so exude it. take inspiration from carrie bradshaw in a midi tulle skirt and t-shirt, and holly golightly in a bedsheet-draped gown, up-do and bare feet: pair something ridiculously fabulous with something utilitarian. what good is throwing a party at home if you can't wear something a little above and beyond? we love skinny jeans and a sequin top, or a floor-length vintage dress with freshly pedicured bare feet; jewel-encrusted flats with a silk blouse and trousers. or pull together a more traditional "perfect" outfit, then throw it off a bit: remove one accessory. add a shocking dash of color. mix a piece of menswear into your feminine attire.

an hour before everyone arrives, make time to sit and have a glass of wine[6] in your ensemble. above all, you want to be comfortable. your guests are there to see you.

[6] "me time" improves your mood, your focus, your decisions; it also helps you relax and provides a sense of accomplishment.

hostess gown, dashiki, kaftan, déshabillé. where there is entertaining, there is most likely a hostess dressed in some very glamorous equivalent of pajamas. light fabrics, bold prints, bright hues, floor-sweeping hemlines and elevated or nonexistent waistlines are the threads that connect the many iterations of the hostess gown over the years, around the world. whatever your personal style, the simple idea of wearing an effortless frock—be it maxi, midi or mini—feels so modern.

the outfit is the outfit.*

wrong always right

*if it makes you feel fabulous.
should you be dressed in a
striped shirt and overalls and
your friends come clad in
suits and dresses, no matter.
your house, your whims.*

movies for
outfit inspiration

▶ *the way we were:* all the high notes from the 1970s: jumpsuits, bell-bottoms and a revolving wardrobe of hats.

▶ *factory girl:* mod mini dresses, furry coats and shoulder-duster earrings.

▶ *to catch a thief:* the feminine silhouettes of the 1950s define grace kelly as an american heiress on vacation.

▶ *breathless:* effortless french gamine: cigarette pants, ballet flats, cat-eye sunglasses, striped dresses and knit tees.

▶ *the graduate:* elegant upper-class 1960s swank: those black dresses. the lingerie! that leopard coat!

▶ *an education:* a crescendo of opulent hues and ladylike silhouettes as the film progresses.

▶ *the talented mr. ripley:* crisp white button-downs; full, feminine midi skirts and flats.

▶ *in the mood for love:* the collection of simply cut dresses in immaculately lush silks is the third star of this film.

▶ *breakfast at tiffany's:* a little black dress is always appropriate.

how to apply bright lipstick

1
if you're concerned about wayward lines, start by applying a thin layer of concealer just around the edge of your lip line. blend into skin.

2
apply lipstick straight from the tube.

3
using a lip liner in the same color as the lipstick, touch up only where the edges aren't perfect— lining the whole lip can look a touch harsh.

4
to make the lipstick last longer, blot with a tissue and then apply a second coat to add back sheen and finish.

add a touch of blush
lightly dab a touch of the same red lipstick on the apples of your cheeks and blend out till sheer for an old hollywood look.

"be **faithful to**
your
own taste,

because nothing

you really like

is ever

art of

style."

BILLY BALDWIN*

*the interior designer famed in the 1950s for his timeless designs, rich use of color and belief
that the client's personal taste in turn enhanced his work for them. not the actor.

care to dance?

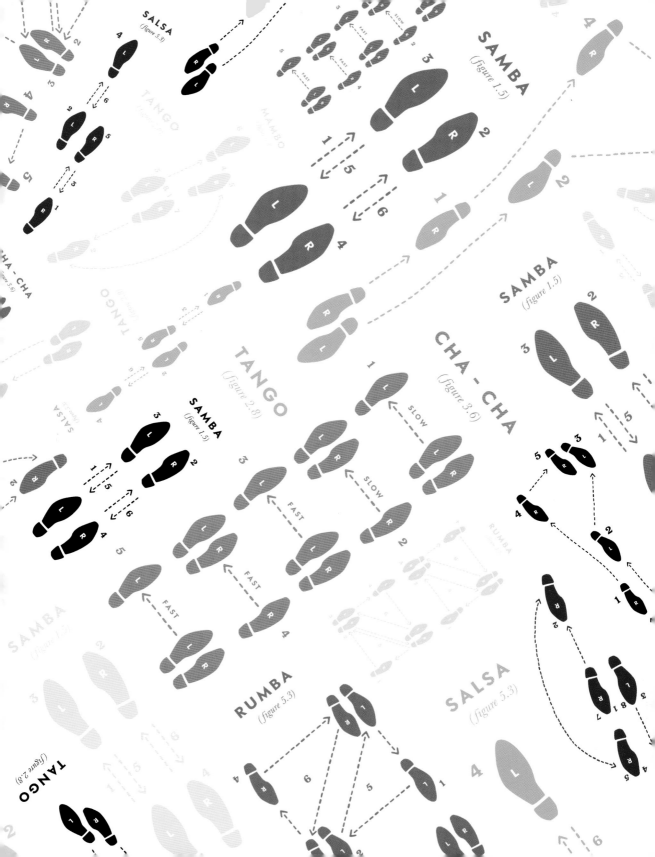

seventy-two words that make everything sound *marvelous*

airy	lacquered
billowy	lavish
charming	layered
chatoyant	lissome
cheeky	luminous
conflate	magical
dalliance	masterful
daring	mellifluous
decadent	natty
delicate	nonchalant
desultory	nubby
diaphanous	opulent
discerning	parenthetical
distinguished	pedigreed
dramatic	plethora
dreamy	polished
dulcet	punchy
effervescent	quintessentially
eloquent	raffish
ephemeral	redolent
ethereal	regal
exquisite	saturated
fanciful	sculptural
fantastical	sensuous
felicity	serendipitous
fetching	serene
furtive	shimmering
genteel	sinewy
gleaming	spirited
glossy	studied
grand	sublime
halcyon	sumptuous
handsome	surreptitious
imbue	svelte
impresario	textural
incipient	voluptuous

*style is
knowing who you are,
what you want to say,*
and **not
giving
a damn.**

GORE VIDAL

WHY DON'T I...

INSPIRING RESOURCES

she tuck
coral
away
floated
to

ed her
lipstick
&
back
the party.

sources

013 pynchon quote: pynchon, thomas. *v.* new york city: J.B. Lippincott Company. 1961.

014 jackie kennedy's flowers: national first ladies library. "first ladies' favorite flowers." *firstladies.org.* 2015.

018-019 the bad and the beautiful quote: *the bad and the beautiful.* dir: vincente minnelli. metro-gold-wyn-mayer, 1952. film.

022 bronfman quote: bronfman, hannah. "hannah bronfman's 15 tips to craft a killer playlist." *cosmopolitan.com.* 23 november 2014.

034-037 woolf quotes: woolf, virginia. *mrs. dalloway.* san diego: harcourt, inc. 1925.

042 beaton quote: garner, philippe and mellor, david alan. *the essential cecil beaton: photographs 1920-1970.* widenmayer-str: schirmer/mosel. 2012.

050 haskins quote: rannals, lee. "how iPhone 5s affects the photography industry: exclusive." *redorbit.com.* 20 september 2013.

051 winogrand quote: halle, howard. "garry winogrand." *time out new york.* 3 september 2014.

051 turgenev quote: turgenev, ivan s. *fathers and sons.* russia: the russian messenger, 1862.

052 sokolsky quote: pepper, terrence; muir, robin; sokolsky, melvin. *twiggy: a life in photographs.* washington, d.c.: national portrait gallery publications, 2009.

052 brooke astor's guest book: sotheby's. "property from the estate of brooke astor." *sothebys.com.* 24 september 2012.

063 bashir quote: carter, stinson. "a day in the life of ruzwana bashir." *the wall street journal.* 27 june 2013.

066 maxwell quote: davis, deborah. *party of the century: the fabulous story of truman capote and his black and white ball.* hoboken: wiley publishing. 2006.

075 de wolfe quote: armour, katie. "the 10 best elsie de wolfe quotes." *matchbook magazine.* matchbook magazine, LLC., 4 june 2013.

089 lebowitz quote: lebowitz, fran. *the fran lebowitz reader.* new york city: vintage books. 1974.

089 child quote: albers, dr. susan. "four fabulous lessons on eating from julia child." *huffingtonpost.com.* 19 august 2013.

089 beard quote: patent, greg. *the french cook - souffles.* layton: gibbs smith. 2014.

089 olney quote: deschenes, steff. *eat the year: 366 fun and fabulous food holidays to celebrate every day.* philadelphia: running press. 2014.

089 beethoven quote: weinstein, jay. *a cup of comfort cookbook.* avon: adams media. 2002.

091 cobb salad: kapoor, tarun. "the classic cobb salad." *gulftimes.com.* 12 february 2015.

094 schiaparelli quote: applewhite, ashton; evans, tripp; frothingham, evan. *and i quote: the definitive collection of quotes, sayings, and jokes for the contemporary speechmaker.* new york city: st. martin's press. 1992.

097 brillat-savarin quote: americana editorial staff. *the americana supplement: a comprehensive record of the latest knowledge and progress of the world.* whitefish: kessinger publishing, 2010.

098 walken quote: Akbar, Arifa. "christopher walken on life and death in hollywood." *the independent.* 20 february 2010.

104 jackson & levine list: courtesy of *jacksonandlevine.co.uk.*

108 van horne quote: van horne, harriet. "six recipes, simple, honest, and sometimes unconventional." *vogue.* 1956.

115 shakespeare quote: shakespeare, william. *twelfth night (folger shakespeare library).* new york city: simon & schuster, 2004.

122 myhrvold quote: myhrvold, nathan. *modernist cuisine: the art and science of cooking.* bellevue: the cooking lab, 2011.

124 hepburn quote: the independent. "audrey hepburn in quotes." *the independent.* 04 may 2014.

136 july quote: july, miranda. *no one belongs here more than you: stories.* new york city: scribner. 2007.

137 loren quote: jet. "words of the week." *jet.* september 1964.

140 communication fact: thompson, jeff. "is nonverbal communication a numbers game?" *psychology today.* 30 september 2011.

142 woolf quote: woolf, virginia. *a room of one's own.* london: hogarth press, 1929.

142 adams quote: ravichandar, hema. "decoding lunchtime at work." *livemint.* 30 december 2012.

147 dunham quote: heller, nathan. "lena dunham: the new queen of comedy's first vogue cover." *vogue,* february 2014.

150-151 parker quote: capron, marion. "dorothy parker, the art of fiction no. 13." *the paris review,* summer 1956.